ONE MAGICAL SUNDAY

ONE MAGICAL SUNDAY
(But Winning Isn't Everything)

PHIL MICKELSON
WITH DONALD T. PHILLIPS

WARNER BOOKS

NEW YORK   BOSTON

Warner Books

Time Warner Book Group
1271 Avenue of the Americas, New York, NY 10020
Visit our Web site at www.twbookmark.com.

Printed in the United States of America

First Edition: April 2005
10   9   8   7   6   5   4   3   2   1

Library of Congress Cataloging-in-Publication Data

Mickelson, Phil
   One magical Sunday : but winning isn't everything / Phil Mickelson
with Donald T. Phillips.—1st ed.
      p.   cm.
      ISBN 0-446-57857-6—ISBN 0-446-57863-0 (large print)
      1. Mickelson, Phil, 1970–   2. Golfers—United States—Biography.
3. Masters Golf Tournament (2004)—Personal narratives.
I. Phillips, Donald T. (Donald Thomas), 1952–   II. Title.

GV964.M53A3   2005
796.352'092—dc22

                                 2005000389

Foreword

I remember it like it was yesterday.

Phil Mickelson standing over his 18-foot putt on the 18th green at Augusta National. If he makes it, he wins the Masters by one shot. It would be his first major tournament victory. I found myself on the edge of my seat, holding my breath.

He stroked his putt. The ball rolled slowly, slowly, ever so slowly toward the hole. At the last moment, it looked like the ball was going to tail off to the left and miss. Instead, it caught the lip on the left side, rolled around to the right side, and dropped into the cup.

Phil jumped into the air, arms extended over his head. The Masters crowd went wild. They also raised their arms in the air. At home, I stood up and screamed, "Yes! Yes!" Tears were streaming down my face and I didn't completely know why.

Later, I found out that people all over the country reacted the same way. They spilled out of airport bars yelling, "He did it! He did it!" They celebrated in department stores, restaurants, hotels, and golf clubhouses. People working in their yards heard shouts of joy coming from their neighbors' homes. When Phil made that putt, there was a collective "hurrah" across the entire nation. It was one of the most thrilling and magic moments in the history of sports.

Several months later, my editor at Warner called. "Don, do you follow golf?" he asked.

"Sure, Rick. I love golf."

"Would you be willing to work with Phil Mickelson on a book?"

I caught the next plane to San Diego.

Don Phillips
Christmas 2004

Warmup

As in life, golf is a game of circles.

I'm on the practice green, walking in circles around the hole. Ten golf balls are spread out eighteen inches apart, in a perfect circle, each exactly three feet away from the cup. I just move around the circle rolling them in—with the same stroke, the same stance, the same setup.

When I knock in five balls, Bones (my caddy) picks them out of the hole and sets them back in the circle behind me. There are a number of people watching and each time I make a putt, I can hear some of them quietly counting—91, 92, 93, 94. . . .

This is part of my pre-tournament routine—one that had been recommended to me by one of the greatest putters the game has ever known—1956 Masters champion Jackie Burke. In this drill, I hit three-foot putts until I make 100 in a row. Ten golf balls. Ten times around the circle. 100 golf balls. But if I miss, I have to start all over again. It may take me only 100 putts if I do it the first time, or it may take 1,500 putts if I keep missing.

That's what happened to me on this past Wednesday's practice session. I kept missing late in my count. "90, 91, 92," the people counted out loud. Then I missed and they groaned. So I started over again. "1, 2, 3. . . ."

I got up into the 90s again. "93, 94, 95," And I missed again. "Oh, noooooo," a couple of guys whispered. "1, 2, 3 . . . " Then I went all the way around again. "97, 98, 99," and I missed the 100th putt.

It kept happening that way. I missed a bunch of times when I was in the 90s, which caused this routine to take forever. I'd much rather miss earlier in the count than late. Golfers who had teed off on their front nine when I started were finishing the 9th hole—and I was still walking around in circles on the putting green. The 1976 Masters champion, Raymond Floyd, looked on for a few minutes. He saw me miss and said, "Man, this is brutal." Then he walked away, unable to watch any longer.

I kept missing on Wednesday. But not today. Today I make the first 100 practice putts. The few who know what I'm doing applaud. And I start my next drill.

It's Sunday morning, April 11, 2004. We're at Augusta National Country Club in Augusta, Georgia. We're going to play the final round of the greatest golf tournament in the world—the Masters.

The Masters: the one tournament with a timeless quality. The only one of the four majors that stays in one place. The others rotate yearly. Not the Masters. It's always played right here on the same golf course—where the legends of golf once stood at the same tee boxes, walked the same fairways, putted on the same greens. Bobby Jones. Walter Hagen. Gene Sarazen. Byron Nelson. Ben Hogan. Sam Snead. In one way or another, they're all here for the 68th Masters. It's Tiger Woods' 10th, Fred Couples' 20th, Tom Watson's 31st, Raymond Floyd's 40th, Jack Nicklaus' 44th, and Arnold Palmer's 50th. I've dreamed about winning this tournament since I was nine years old. And now I'm getting my 12th shot at it.

You'll never play a round of golf in a more beautiful setting. The tall pines, the azaleas, the lush green fairways, the velvet greens. Each hole is named for a flower, a plant, a tree, or a bush that surrounds that particular fairway or green. There seems to be a real sense of calmness across the golf course today. The color of the leaves, the smell of the grass. The air, the light, the sun, the feeling. It's hard to explain. This place is just magical. Today's weather is sunny and cloudless with mild temperatures. There are some light winds and conditions are dry. The course will play firm and fast. It'll be a great day to play golf.

During Thursday's first round, we had a two-hour rain delay. Then things cleared up nicely. Actually, I wouldn't have minded at all if the rain had kept up—as long as we could continue playing. When it rains, the ball doesn't run as much once it hits the ground. Since I have a tendency to hit my shots higher and carry them more, I thought it would be an advantage for me. Also, when I was a kid, I'd go to this par 3 golf course near my home. Rainy days were my favorite times because nobody else would be there. So I'd put on my rain gear, grab a bucket of balls, and go out under a palm tree. I'd have the entire place as my private driving range—free to hit the ball wherever I wished. I loved how peaceful and calm it was. One time, it really started to pour and one of my friends who worked in the pro shop came out and asked me what in the world I was doing. "This extra practice, right here, is going to help me win a couple of Masters someday," I responded. That's a true story.

My wife, Amy, and our three children are with me this week. So are my mom, dad, and sister—as are Amy's parents. It's nice to have everybody here, especially today, Easter Sunday. Last night, Amy and I helped the Easter Bunny hide the children's Easter baskets. When Amanda, Sophia, and Evan woke up this morning, they had to follow a trail of jellybeans all over the place—under couches, over tables, behind curtains. It was a lot of fun watching them. Right now they're all back at the house coloring Easter eggs. I know Amanda, especially, was looking forward to that.

It's funny, there are a lot of things I recall from my child-hood—but one Easter weekend was especially memorable. It was then that I learned that playing golf was not a right, but a very special privilege.

―――――

When Philip was eleven years old, he failed to do his chores around the house. As a boy, he didn't generally do things that were wrong. He just sometimes didn't do the things he was supposed to do.

Well, there were three junior golf events that particular Easter weekend, and Philip's punishment was that he could not play in them. He moped around the house all weekend, but he learned a good lesson.

After that, we never really had too many problems with our son. He knew that golf would be taken away from him if he misbehaved in any way. And that was the last thing he wanted to have happen. I mean, it was pure torture for Philip not to be able to play golf.

Mary and Philip Mickelson, Sr., Phil's Parents

―――――

I showed up at the golf course by 10:00 a.m. this morning. Whenever I have a late tee time, as I do today, I use a double warm-up routine that helps me prepare for the day without expending too much energy. I begin with a one- to two-hour practice session at the driving range to work on distance control with my irons—and by that I mean, if I have to hit a shot 132 yards, I do not hit it 137 yards. Given the severity of the greens, a slight miscalculation can mean the difference between birdie and bogey. Then I go over to the practice putting green and, after I make my 100 three-foot putts, I'll take an hour off and eat a good lunch.

At my lunch break today, I changed my shirt from white to black. I usually try to practice in a white shirt because it's cooler and usually matches whatever pants I have on that day. Amy usually picks out what I wear. As a matter of fact, I consult with her on my entire wardrobe because I have zero fashion sense—and I've learned the hard way that I can really get burned if I'm not careful.

When I was a senior in high school, for instance, I qualified as an amateur for the San Diego Open. It was my first real PGA Tour experience and I was very excited. I wanted to dress like the pros so, on Thursday, I wore my coolest pair of yellow polyester pants and a green-striped, hard-collared shirt. I looked *good*! Or so I thought.

In the middle of the round, my playing partner (who was in his first year on the Tour) was up in the fairway getting ready to hit his shot, so I stood behind him, still as can be, and tried to be quiet. I guess my outfit distracted him, because he said, "Hey, Phil, would you mind moving just a little bit. It wouldn't normally be a problem, but today you look like a *freaking* canary!" (That's the G-rated version!)

Ooooo, that one hurt because all my friends and family were there, looking on. When I got to Arizona State University the next year, the other members of the golf team took me right down to the mall and made me buy khaki pants and shirts with soft collars.

Philip developed his fashion sense at a very early age. When he was four years old, we sent him to a weeklong golf clinic, and on the last day, he was to compete in a big putting contest against everybody else—including some teenagers.

Well, he was a golfer now and wanted to dress himself for this very important event. We said okay, so he put on a pair of plaid pants and a striped shirt. Then he went out and won that little tournament and brought home his very first trophy (which he slept with that night). And wouldn't you know it, the next morning, Philip's picture was in the local paper—in his glowing outfit holding his new trophy!

Mary and Philip Mickelson, Sr.

When I emerge from the clubhouse with my "Outfit by Amy," I go to the driving range and tune up with some long- and short-iron shots. Then I head back to the practice green and start working on some longer putts. I especially hit a lot of 15- to 20-footers just because, typically, that's the distance you've got to putt to make birdies at Augusta National.

As I wind up my practice session, a lot of nice people are saying encouraging words. "This is your year, Phil." "Make this your first one. We're pulling for you." They are not talking about me winning my first PGA Tournament. I've already won 22 Tour events. They're talking about me winning my first major.

There are four major golf tournaments—the Masters, the U. S. Open, the British Open, and the PGA Championship. This will be my 47th major tournament. My first was the U. S. Open in 1990. I've finished in the top ten sixteen times, but never won. I've finished in third place in three of the last four Masters—including the last three years in a row. The media has blessed me with the title: "The Best Player Never to Have Won a Major Championship." Jack Nicklaus has won the most professional majors—eighteen. Tiger Woods has already won eight. Ben Hogan won nine. Arnold Palmer, seven. Byron Nelson 5. "What's wrong with me?" I keep hearing.

I've come close over the years—real close. In 1999, Payne Stewart holed a long putt at the U. S. Open to beat me by a shot. David Toms did the same thing at the PGA Championship in 2001. And I was runner-up to Tiger at the 2002 U. S. Open. Some people say I seem to "choke" at the big events. Others say that I'm too aggressive, that I "go for it" too often when I should be more conservative and lay up. Still others simply call me "golf's most lovable runner-up." With every year that passes, it seems there is more and more emphasis placed on this "major" statistic. I remember one headline from a national newspaper just before 1999's PGA Championship: "Last Chance for Phil Mickelson to Win a Major Tournament Before the Millennium Ends."

For whatever reason, it's been more difficult for me to win major championships than regular tour events. I'd like to win one. But I don't think I would be a different player if I did. And I certainly don't look at myself as a failure in any way. In that case, I would dread these major tournaments—rather than look forward to them as I do every year. Actually I like the challenge because I truly believe that success is more rewarding when it is difficult to achieve.

My entire family is excited at this year's Masters because I'm tied for the lead after three rounds. I've had rounds of 72, 69, and

69. I haven't made a bogey since the 4th hole of Friday's round. That's 32 holes in a row at par or better. Not bad for some, but amazing for me. I'm driving the ball well and hitting greens in regulation. All in all, I've had a great tournament to this point.

But winning my first green jacket (the traditional award for a Masters champion) won't be an easy thing to accomplish. I'm competing against an international field with some of the finest golfers from America and all over the world. Here's how the leaderboard stacks up as we begin our last round:

PLAYER	SCORE
Phil Mickelson	−6
Chris DiMarco	−6
Paul Casey	−4
Ernie Els	−3
Bernhard Langer	−3
K. J. Choi	−3
Kirk Triplett	−2
Davis Love III	−1
Fredrik Jaacobson	−1
Vijay Singh	E
Fred Couples	E
Retief Goosen	E
Jay Haas	E
Padraig Harrington	E
Nick Price	E

Despite the tough competition, I like my chances today for a number of reasons. First, this is the only time I've ever had the lead (or been tied for the lead) going into the last round of a major. Because I don't have to make up ground on the leaders, I'm not going to have to play flawless golf today.

Second, I'm paired with a good friend of mine, Chris Di-Marco. We've played together many times before—going all the way back to college when I was at Arizona State and Chris was at Florida. He and I are tied for the lead and clearly, he's also having a great tournament. Although Chris and I will be competing today, our friendship and his sense of humor should ease some of the tension and pressure.

The third reason I feel good about my chances is that I've really prepared for this event. Last week, I walked the course with Rick Smith (my long-game coach) and Dave Pelz (my short-game coach) trying to find areas where I could shave off a shot or two from my rounds. Also, in my previous eleven Masters, I've become very familiar with the golf course. I know Augusta National inside and out. I've learned the nuances of the course through practice rounds with many of the past Masters champions. I've learned where you can get up and down from off the green to make par. I know which pin placements you can attack, and which ones you should be more cautious toward. I know where you can chip around the greens, and where you should putt instead. I've studied every single green for shot dispersion, speed, and break. This course, I believe, sets up well for me as a left-handed golfer.

Having my friends and family around makes me more determined. Steve Loy, my former college coach and current business manager, is here. So are Dave Pelz and Rick Smith, who, because they know Sunday at the Masters can put a lot of pressure on a golfer, are trying to help me to relax.

PHIL MICKELSON

Phil was really tuned in during his morning practice session. In fact, he didn't make a bad swing at all. It was a teacher's dream to see him performing so well. There just wasn't anything technical or analytical to discuss. So I tried to make sure he was relaxed.

About a half-hour before he was due to tee off, Phil started talking about solar eclipses and spiral galaxies. At that point, I figured he was relaxed enough.

Rick Smith, Phil's Long-Game Coach

Rick's wife, Tricia (who is a vegetarian and has not broken her diet for over a decade), told me that if I were to win the Masters today, she would eat meat. Maybe that kind of motivation is why Rick put in so many long hours with me. Dave Pelz also reminded me again that I often seem too serious on Sundays. So I've decided to take it easy today and try to have a good time.

Overall, I'm heading into the final round of this major more at ease that I ever have been in the past. I don't feel the usual anxiety. Actually, I haven't felt any all year. Last night, Amy and I talked at length about it. We were just very calm. We felt things were different. For some reason, we both had a belief that I was going to come through—that today was going to be one magical Sunday.

ONE MAGICAL SUNDAY

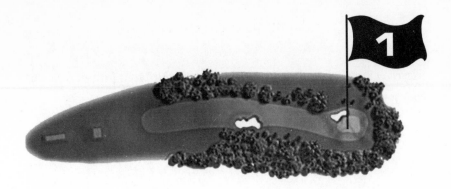

Tea Olive
Par 4
435 yards
Slight Dogleg Right

*S*tepping onto the first tee, I shake hands with the marshal in the green jacket and he hands me Chris DiMarco's scorecard. I keep my partner's score, he keeps mine. Chris and I then have a brief conversation about what brand and number balls we are going to play.

I'm pretty calm and looking forward to the day. But I want to get off a decent first shot. Most golfers typically don't play the first four holes very well. They try to hit the ball too hard, often miss the fairway, and end up making bogeys. They have to fight back in the middle of the round and then their scores improve. I'm determined not to go out too hard so that doesn't happen.

Chris has the honors and hits first. "Fore, please," says the marshal. "Chris DiMarco now driving." He drives it in the bunker on the right side of the fairway—not a good place to be. Now it's my turn.

"Fore, please. Phil Mickelson now driving."

There is some applause. I tip my visor, take a couple of practice swings, then stand behind my ball and look down the fairway. Unknown to me, the *television broadcast is flashing a graphic up on the screen (just in case anybody forgets):*

Most Career Wins WITHOUT A MAJOR	
Harry Cooper	41
MacDonald Smith	24
Phil Mickelson	22

The key to the first hole is the fairway bunker on the right. It's a 300-yard carry and I don't want to risk flying over it because I'll be left with a very tough shot (just as DiMarco has). I just want to hit it in the fairway. So I'm going to make sure that, if I miss it, I miss it left—even though driving too far to the left may catch the trees. One thing I've worked on all year, however, is taking the right side out of play. I decide to hit a fade (right to left for a left-handed golfer). It's a tight shot for me.

As I step up to the ball, my feet are aimed directly at the bunker. I hit the ball well, but I actually fade it a bit too far (a rush of adrenaline, I guess). The ball takes a huge bounce to the left, plunks against a tree trunk, bounces back, and comes to rest in some pine straw. I think I'll be okay. I should have a shot to the green.

As I walk off the first tee, I'm not overly nervous or excited. I'm looking forward to the day.

Okay, here we go. This is the beginning.

On June 16, 1970, my parents sent out an interesting birth announcement. On the front cover, there was a sketch of a baby with a golf bag slung over his shoulder and a golf green with a little yellow flagstick stuck in it. "Introducing the Mickelsons' 'fourth,'" it said. Inside, the announcement read as follows:

> Philip Alfred hurried to join the Mickelson threesome on the first tee at Mercy Hospital for a 3:45 p.m. starting time on June 16, 1970. Using all of his 8 lbs, 13 ounces in a powerful swing, Philip proudly equaled his height with a tee shot of 21 inches. Philip's first message: "Let's play golf at my new home in San Diego."

As you might be able to guess, golf was my father's passion in life. Dad was also a top athlete in his day—an Olympic caliber snow skier, a competition water skier, and a gymnast. He was a fighter pilot in the Navy, flew with the Blue Angels, and was an instructor for the best pilots in the service. Dad also had a teaching degree, but when I was born he was a pilot for a major airline. People tell me that I get my analytical mind from my him—and my sense of humor from my mother. Mom was a nurse and ran her own health care business. She's always been very intuitive, incredibly fun, and just loves practical jokes. My sister, Tina, was nearly two when I was born. And seven years later, my brother, Tim, was born. That completed our immediate family. But our extended family was much bigger—with lots of grandparents, uncles, aunts, and cousins. And everybody lived in San Diego.

When I was about 18 months old, and starting to walk fairly well, my dad would take me out into the back yard while he chipped golf balls (we had a good-sized back yard). He would stand near the house in this little area that he had fashioned to look like a tee box. In order to keep an eye on me, he'd sit me down right across from him—just far enough out of range of the clubs. I'd sit there and play with the golf balls. And when my dad would run out, I was reluctant to give him another one to hit because I liked playing with them so much. When all the balls were gone, we'd go get them all, come back, and I'd watch my dad chip them again.

We did that together for about three or four months—my dad chipping and me sitting right across from him watching. Then, just before I turned two, he cut down a right-handed wood short enough for me to swing. Then he had me stand in front of him, and set me up to hit the ball. "Okay, Philip," he said stepping back. "Now, you can hit it."

"Yay!" I said excitedly. Then I went across to my spot, re-gripped the club left-handed, and took a whack at the ball.

My father is one of the most patient men I've ever met—and I think it comes naturally to him. "Well, that was a pretty good swing," he said, "but we've got a right-handed club, so come back over here."

So he set me up again and said: "Okay, go ahead and hit it." And I went right back over to the other side and hit it left-handed again. It just seemed more natural for me to hit the ball left-handed. Besides, I really wanted to be the mirror image of my dad. And he will tell you that my swing was so fundamentally sound that he decided not to mess around with it. "We'll just change the golf club instead," he told my mom.

He took the club over to his workbench and, by sawing and grinding for a while, turned the back into the front and the front into the back. After finishing and lacquering it, I now had my new favorite toy (a left-handed kids club)—and I absolutely wore it out. (By the way, I've always been naturally right-handed. Virtually the only thing I do left-handed is swing a golf club.)

My mom tells me that, at this age, I was just mesmerized with my golf balls. At night before I went to sleep, I'd arrange them just so on my bed, and then I'd sleep with them—along with Flopsy, my stuffed dog, and my special blanket. When I woke up in the morning, the first thing I wanted to do was go out in the back yard and hit my golf balls. So I'd be trying to carry all these golf balls down the stairs and they would fall out of my arms and go bounding down the stairs to the floor. And the sound of those bouncing golf balls was how my mom always knew I was awake and out of bed each morning.

By age three and a half, I had learned that the night before my dad was going to play golf, he would stand his golf bag next to the front door. Well, when he'd get up the next morning, he'd find my little set of four clubs next to his because I would put them there on purpose. Then I'd go up to him and ask: "Dad, can I go with you to the big golf course and play?" But he always said no because he didn't think there was a chance of ever being able to get a kid so young on the course.

After asking to go along a bunch of times—and always receiving the same answer—I decided that if they weren't going to let me play golf, I was going to run away from home. So I enlisted my little buddy next door, Chris Peters—and one morning we just took off. I slung my little golf bag over my shoulder, picked up Flopsy and my favorite blanket, grabbed my tiny suitcase (which was filled with nothing more than golf balls) and headed down the street with Chris.

Chris's mom saw us and immediately called one of the neighbors, Anita Philpot. "You know," she said, "I think Chris and Philip have run away from home. And I think they're going to the golf course."

So Mrs. Philpot came outside and asked us where we were going.

"We ran away from home!" I said. "And, ummm, we're going to the golf course."

"I see," she said.

"Mrs. Philpot?" I said.

"Yes, Philip?"

"How do we get to the golf course?"

"Well, you go down to the corner here and you turn left and just keep following that road."

"Thanks, Mrs. Philpot. Bye."

It turned out that the road Mrs. Philpot advised us to take just went around in a big circle and led us right back to my house. And of course, both our mothers were waiting for us in the driveway.

After that episode, my dad had a change of heart about taking me to the big golf course.

If Philip wanted to be on the big golf course that bad, then I figured we should at least try to get him on. Besides, I didn't want to see him run away again.

Phil Mickelson, Sr., Phil's Dad

So the next weekend, when my dad, my grandfather, and one of their friends went to play golf, I tagged along as the last member of the foursome. When we got to the golf course, they all had to do some pretty fast talking.

"Yes, he has his own golf clubs."

"Yes, he can keep up."

"No, he won't get tired."

"No, he won't run away from us."

Finally the manager at Balboa Municipal Golf Course said, "Okay, he can play."

At the first hole, I'd hit the ball a little ways down the fairway. Then I'd pick up my tiny four-club golf bag, run up to the ball, set my clubs down, hit the ball again, pick up my clubs, and run off again.

After two holes of this, I turned to my father. "Dad," I said, "can you carry these clubs for me? It's just taking too much time to pick them up and put them down." And he said: "Sure, I can do that."

So for the entire round, that's the way it went. I was running and hitting, running and hitting, running and hitting—until we got to the middle of the 18th fairway. This hole was a long par five and the rest of the way was all uphill. In fact, this stretch was such a long, tiring uphill walk that the golfers had nicknamed it "Cardiac Hill." It was at this point I stopped and looked up at my dad.

"Dad," I said, "I don't want to play this hole?"

"Why don't you want to play?" he asked.

"Isn't this the last hole?"

"Yes."

"Well, if we play this hole, then we'll be all done."

My son didn't want to play the 18th hole, not because he was tired, as I first assumed, but simply because he did not want to be finished with our round of golf. Of course, I told him that we had to play it—and he ran right up Cardiac Hill in front of us with the same amount of energy he'd shown all day long.

And I remember thinking to myself: "This kid is just *destined* to play golf."

Phil Mickelson, Sr.

My drive off the #1 tee has come to rest in the pine needles about three feet to the right of the tree it hit. But the ball is sitting up nicely and, because I'm a lefty, I have plenty of room for my stance. If I were right-handed, I'd have a real problem on this shot. I've got 127 yards to the green and I can see the flag.

Usually, the officials at Augusta National put the pin on the top shelf or in the back of the green. But today, they have it on the right side in a low area. It's in a perfect spot to make birdie because all the balls will funnel right down to the hole. Interestingly enough, most of the pin placements have been set up for potential birdies today. The course is not going to play as tough as it did during Thursday's first round. I guess Augusta officials wanted to see some fireworks today. And the pin placement on #1 is set up to get the guys off to a quick start.

My only problem with this shot is a couple of low hanging tree limbs right in front of me. Rather than hit the ball in a big arcing circle around them, I decide to take a 6 iron, hit a low chip-runner, and go under the limbs. And I hit a terrific shot—on the green only twelve feet from the hole.

I've played this pin position only one other time in competition and, as I'm lining up the putt, I'm unsure of just how far it will break. Sure enough, it breaks a little bit more than I judge. I miss it to the right by a half an inch and leave it a foot from the hole. Then I tap in for a par 4.

I'm not nervous or overly concerned. It was a chance for me to get off to a good start—but I have a couple of par fives coming up that I can birdie.

Chris DiMarco made a great shot out of the fairway bunker and also parred the hole. We're still tied for the lead. Here's how things stand after #1.

PLAYER	SCORE	HOLE
Phil Mickelson	–6	1
Chris DiMarco	–6	1
Bernhard Langer	–5	2
Ernie Els	–4	2
Paul Casey	–4	2
K. J. Choi	–3	2
Vijay Singh	–1	6
Nick Price	–1	5
Kirk Triplett	–1	3
Davis Love III	E	6

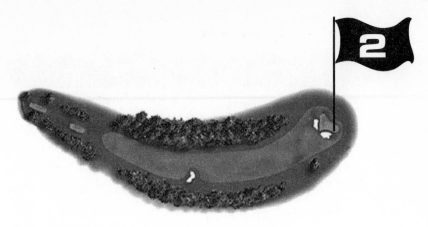

Pink Dogwood
Par 5
575 yards
Dogleg Left

*T*his is one of the toughest driving holes at Augusta. A very tight, right to left hole—but the green is reachable in two. Definitely an opportunity to make birdie. I must be careful, however. In last year's final round, I hit it in the hazard, took a penalty stroke, and turned a likely bogey into a miraculous birdie. I don't want to tempt fate again. There's a bunker on the right side of the fairway here also—about 300 yards out. I'm going to aim right at it and hit a little fade.

My swing feels good and the ball does just what I want it to do. It travels 300 yards and lands right in the middle of the fairway. When I get out there, I notice, once again, that there is an easy pin placement— back right in a low spot. It's downhill and 269 yards to the hole. I can make it with a three-wood. But I don't want to miss this shot to the right because it's a much more difficult up and down from there. So I've just got to be left. There are two very deep front greenside bunkers on this hole. I'm going to aim at the one on the right side, try to cut the ball (a sharp right-to-left fade) so that it lands right in the middle of the green, *and let it funnel down to the hole. If it goes in the bunker, it won't be a problem. It's not a difficult shot.*

My swing feels really good, but I hit the ball too long and too far to the left. It rolls off the green and into the first row of spectators. Not my best effort. Now I have a tough shot to get up and down for birdie. My playing partner, Chris DeMarco, with whom I'm tied for the lead, is in good shape, though. He's got a pretty easy chip shot and probably will make birdie.

Walking down the fairway to the second green, I'm thinking I want to have fun today. I'm going to enjoy working with Bones, my caddy. And I'm going to make an effort to talk to Chris.. I don't want this day to be heavy and intense. I want it to be light. I want to have fun.

When I was eight years old, my father and I were playing an afternoon nine-hole round of golf—as we often did after I got out of school. On one of the early holes, I made a bad shot and slammed my club on the ground in disgust. Dad looked at me kind of funny and must have thought to himself, "Gee, I've never seen that before." When it happened again a couple of shots later, he stopped me. "Philip, what's going on here?" he asked. "You look like you're not having fun. You're banging your golf club—and it looks like you don't want to play."

"Nahh, I'm having fun, Dad," I said.

"Well, that doesn't look very nice. And it sure looks like you're not having fun. If we're out here on the golf course, this is supposed to be fun. Don't do that anymore. And if you damage your clubs, don't look for me to replace them."

So we played several more holes and, on the 7th green, I missed a putt and slammed my club down again.

"Philip, you're obviously not having fun," said my dad. "So put your golf clubs in your golf bag. And you can walk along with me until you can start having fun."

Dad then played the 8th hole and I walked along. Well, when he was pulling his ball out of the cup, I reached up and tugged his shirt.

"Dad, I think I can have fun now."

"Okay, Philip. Let's play this last hole together and have fun."

Ever since that day, and through all these years since, I cannot tell from the expression on Philip's face whether he is four over par or four under par.

Phil Mickelson, Sr.

Both my mom and dad will tell you that, in those early years, I was a strong-willed child. If my mom told me to go to the left, I would go to the right. Well, they didn't want to break my spirit, so when I refused to put my napkin on my lap at the dinner table, they took a slightly innovative approach to the problem.

"Okay, you don't have to put your napkin on your lap, Philip," they'd say. "But if we catch you without it on your lap, then no matter where you are—at home, in a restaurant, at a friend's house—you've got to go out somewhere far away and count to ten loud enough for us to hear you."

Well, the first time the family went out to a restaurant after setting up this new rule, my sister, Tina, and I quietly slipped our napkins onto our laps. But Dad forgot. And when he took his first bite, we jumped up and said: "Dad, you have to go count." So my father went outside the restaurant and loudly counted to ten. Tina and I got a kick out of it and kept shouting, "Dad, we can't hear you!"

I felt that I had to go out there and count to ten because, if I didn't, my kids would never learn the importance of honesty, integrity, and doing what you say you are going to do. If the new rule applied to them, then it had to apply to me, too.

Phil Mickelson, Sr.

Over the years, there were a lot of little lessons like that—you know, important principles that my parents would try to teach us when we were young. We went on a lot of family trips, for example—to Disneyland, skiing, boating, and so on. Well, wherever we were, Mom and Dad always tried to quit at the peak of the fun. When skiing, rather than let us wear ourselves out and, at the end of the day, be lying in the snow wet, cold, and tired, we'd leave when we were having the most fun. That way, we always wanted to go back and do it some more. In fact, we begged to go back again. It just added to the anticipation and thrill.

Skiing in the winter was one of our favorite things to do. And my father, who was a great skier, taught me both the skill of skiing and life lessons that went along with the sport. He taught me, for instance, the proper way to fall so I wouldn't hurt myself. But when Tina and I came down from the bunny slope one time and proudly announced that we had not fallen one time on the entire run, Dad looked at us and said: "Then you didn't learn anything, did you?

Unless you're falling once in a while, unless you're pushing the envelope every now and then, you're probably not improving."

Of course the next time we came down the slope, both Tina and I were proudly saying: "Dad! We learned a lot this time! We fell all over the place!"

I had an awesome childhood. All those family trips we took provided life lessons and memories that will last a lifetime. As you might imagine, though, golf was the biggest part of my childhood. I'm so thankful my parents supported and encouraged me along the way.

Shortly before I turned five, Mom took me to a week-long junior golf clinic at one of the local courses. At the end of the first day, the guy who was running the clinic pulled me out in front of the rest of the kids. "Here, watch Phil Mickelson swing," he said. "See how he shifts his weight from back to front. This is the way all of you should do it."

At the end of the week, they held a putting contest for the entire group—including some teenagers. I won that putting contest and took home my first trophy (I slept with it that night). The very next weekend, my mom entered me in the Pee Wee International golf tournament—and I came in second.

By the time I was six, my parents had become good friends with the owners of the Presidio Hills par-3 golf course. And during the summers when they were both at work and I was out of school, my mom would pack a lunch and drop me off there in the morning with five dollars. It would cost $4.50 to play all day and that left me with just enough money to buy two soft drinks—one in the morning and one in the afternoon.

Our friends there kept close watch on me when I was out playing golf. As time went by, I got bored with hitting to the same holes all the time—so when nobody was around, I'd hit from the fourth tee to the seventh green, and things like that, just to make it interesting. I'd also put my ball behind trees in order to practice difficult shots. I just loved being out there because it was just the golf course and me. It was at Presidio Hills that I made my first birdie and broke par for the first time. I think I was about seven years old when that happened.

That same year, I earned my first set of golf clubs. My dad and I had this deal. When I finished first or second in a junior golf event, he would buy me a full set of clubs. True to his word, when I finished second at an event in La Jolla, my dad later stopped at a small golf course and went into the pro shop. Left-handed clubs for kids were hard to find. So Dad just asked if they had a used set of ladies' left-handed clubs. Sure enough, they did—and he paid $45 and we took the clubs home. Then he went right to his workbench and cut the shafts down to my size. You know, my dad was pretty smart about getting those ladies' clubs. The shafts were weaker than those on men's clubs and when he reduced the lengths, they actually felt like they were made for me.

After all of that, however, my dad rarely bought me golf clubs. He made me start earning them. So when I was eight, I got a job working at the Navajo Canyon public golf course picking up range balls two or three nights a week. I did that until the age of twelve when new ownership laid off everyone under the age of sixteen.

One of my fondest memories as a kid is playing golf with my father. When he wasn't flying, he'd pick me up from school around three o'clock and we would go out to the Balboa golf course. For only a couple of dollars, we could play until dark. And many times, we'd get stuck out around #13 and #14 because we couldn't see anymore. So we'd have to hike down the mountainous terrain and back up Cardiac Hill to get to the clubhouse. And now, as an adult, every time I drive by that course, I think of my dad and those walks—and the conversations we had along the way.

The Masters golf course at Augusta has a similar terrain. And every now and then, as I would be walking from shot to shot there, it would remind me of those days and evenings with my dad at Balboa.

My second shot on #2 was about five yards off the back left side of the green and I have quite a distance to cover to get to the pin. As I survey the green, I realize I don't need to hit the ball very far but, rather, need it to come in really soft because the slope is steep and fast. So I decide to try a lob shot and fly the ball as close to the hole as I can. If I land it shorter, it will gain momentum down the hill—and I really don't want that to happen. I open the face of my wedge way up and hit a big, long, high, soft shot. But as the ball hits the green, it gains momentum and runs just off the edge into the fringe—a little farther from the hole than I'd like. It turns out there was just no way to get the ball stopped from where I was. I shake my head in bewilderment but, because I'm only 20 feet from the hole, I know I still have a chance to make birdie.

Chipping around Augusta can be difficult. So this year, I've tried to putt when I could. In my pre-tournament preparations, I spent a lot of time practice putting from off the greens because chipping can be tough at Augusta National. Part of the difficulty in chipping is due to the fact that the grass is mowed away from the green—which is opposite of most other courses. As a result, the blades of grass are facing toward you when you chip—and when your ball hits the grass, it has a tendency to slow down or even stop rather than go forward.

So I decide to use my putter. I move the ball slightly up in my stance to give the club more loft so that the ball doesn't get caught by the grass right away. I'm thinking to myself that this is not a hard putt—just a little right to left break. If I get the speed right, I have a good chance to hole it. I make a good stroke and the ball falls right into the cup.

It's nice to start off with a birdie at the first par five. Everybody else who's going to make a run today will probably birdie the second hole. And even though I didn't play it the best, I'm able to walk away with a four and not give up any ground.

Chris DiMarco also made a birdie, though. After the second hole, we're still leading the field by two.

PLAYER	SCORE	HOLE
Mickelson	−7	2
DiMarco	−7	2
Langer	−5	2
Casey	−4	2
Els	−3	3

Flowering Peach
Par 4
350 yards

*T*he third hole at Augusta is a short par four. There are fairway bunkers on the left and you're hitting to an extremely small elevated green. So far, I've played this hole differently each day (depending on where the pin is located). In two of the first three rounds, with the pin back and plenty of green to work with, I was able to use a driver and knock it down to within 50 yards and then chip up. But today, the pin is over in a tiny little area where it is extremely hard to land your ball. If you hit it even a tad too short, it'll roll off the front of the green. And if you hit it just a little too long, it'll roll off the back.

My decision is to hit a 3-iron off the tee and play a low, knockdown, running shot. That way, I'll have a full wedge second shot that I can take high and bring it in to the green more vertically (which will give me a better chance of landing it on the green close to the hole).

My tee shot goes exactly where I want it to go—in the middle of the fairway. I'm sure this surprises the golf analysts. Rarely am I in the top ten in driving accuracy. But this week, I'm hitting it great and am tied for ninth in driving accuracy going into today's round.

For my approach shot, I'm thinking that I have to fly the ball all the way to the hole. I fly it too far, however—about five yards over the green. But I missed it where I had to miss it to make par. There's a ridge between my ball and the pin, so I'll have to go up it and let the ball roll down to the hole.

It's funny. I've had this exact same shot every year that I've played in the Masters. Yet I've never gotten it up and down for par. I've tried chipping it with a sand wedge, hitting it high with a lob wedge, and doing a bump and run with other irons. But I'm really looking forward to this shot to see if I can do better. It's a tough one for me—but, even as a child, I loved challenging shots around the green.

When I was nine or ten years old, my dad built a putting green in the back yard complete with bunker and flagstick. He also mounded the area so we could hit just about any kind of shot that could be envisioned. There were plenty of slopes and, of course, there were trees and bushes all over the place. Beyond the green, there was a rather large canyon. So when we got tired of chipping, we could let some fly out there—maybe up to 150 yards or so. And over the years, we hit garbage cans full of balls out into that canyon. Most of the golf balls were given to us by the local driving ranges before being discarded.

Sometimes, I would play out there by myself all day long and, when we added some lighting, well into the night. After a while, I'd get bored with the same old monotonous shot, so I started moving all around the back yard—around obstacles, under trees, behind bushes, on the side of the bunker, in the sand. And I just kept making shots up like that. I'd go back up against the fence and try to hit the ball on the green. I'd hit it below the tree, above the bush, and out to the flagstick. And then I'd move the pins around. It's easier on this part of the green; harder on that part. Hit it from here and go over the trap. Chip it from a downhill lie, an uphill lie, a flat lie. Put some spin on the ball and see if I can back it up next to the hole.

As I got better and better, my dad would work with me and we'd devise all kinds of different games. For instance, we'd take twenty balls each and, from different places around the green, see how many shots we could knock within a flagstick length of the hole. If we knocked one in the hole, we got two points.

After a while, I began to notice that the ball would react in different ways depending on how my club struck it. So I started to experiment. If I hit it just right, I could make it back up, or bounce right, or bounce left. I could hit it fat and watch it loft very softly— de-loft the club and watch it roll along the ground. I'd hit it below the equator of the ball and above the equator just to see what would happen. Sometimes, my dad and I would try some crazy shots and then talk about why the ball did what it did. It was just fascinating to me.

Before you knew it, I was practicing all kinds of trick shots in the back yard. It got so I could hit the ball high enough in the air to go over a man's head standing three feet in front of me and have it land in a bucket behind him. Usually, I practiced these types of shots when I was home by myself, because they were pretty risky.

I remember one time when I was facing our house and trying to make the ball go in a different direction with a full swing. Well, I hit it wrong and it went flying off to the right at full force and crashed into our neighbor's sliding glass doors. When I heard the glass shatter, I remember thinking, "Oh, no!" I ran back into the house and sure enough, within thirty seconds the phone rang and I answered it. "Hello?" I said.

"Philip," said Mrs. Peters, our next door neighbor, "is your mother home?"

"No, Mrs. Peters, ma'am, she isn't. Is everything okay?"

"Oh, yes, Philip. Everything's fine. I just want to talk to your mother." I remember it took me forever to pay for those new sliding glass doors.

The truth is that I broke a bunch of windows in the Peters house. One time Mr. Peters came home and found one of my golf balls on the floor of an upstairs bedroom. Of course, the window was smashed to pieces. "Hmmm," he said when he called my mother, "I wonder who could have done this." Fortunately, Mr. and Mrs. Peters did not get upset easily.

Despite the occasional broken window, I was improving quickly. And I remember the first time I ever beat my father. I was about ten years old and we were playing a round over at Navajo Canyon. It just so happened on this day that Dad was not playing his best and I was playing as well as I could. He ended up shooting an 81 and I had a 73. I beat him by eight shots and I wanted everyone to know.

Well, when we got home, Dad started messing around in the garage and I was hanging around my mom in the kitchen. But I could not tell her what I had done because of a lesson I remembered from a skiing trip a few years before.

On one of our family trips, we were riding a chairlift up the mountain next to a guy who kept telling us he was the greatest skier in the world. And I remember being real impressed with what he said he could do. But when we got off the lift, the "greatest skier in the world" kept falling flat on his face. It turned out he was a *terrible* skier. And that's when my mom and dad pulled me aside. "You see, Philip," they said, "it just doesn't sound good when you tell a person how great you are or how good you are at something. It just doesn't come across right. It's always better to hear it from somebody else."

So when I got home, I waited until my dad came in from the garage and we were all in the kitchen together. I thought he was going to tell Mom what had happened, but he didn't. And Mom was too busy cooking to ask how our round went. Well, I just couldn't take it anymore, so I finally burst out: "Dad! Aren't you going to tell Mom what happened? C'mon!"

"Oh, yeah," my dad said finally. "Philip beat me for the first time—by eight strokes."

He was just beaming from ear to ear! What a smile! He was so proud of himself at that moment. And yet, he did not want to sound conceited. He just would not tell me himself. It had to be his dad who told me.

Mary Mickelson, Phil's Mom

A few years later, I started playing in junior golf tournaments. I'll always remember my dad driving me all the way to Tucson to play in one two-day event. I had been only a shot or two behind going into the second day, but I ended up shooting an 88 and fell way back.

We had a six-hour drive back home and, instead of laying into me (like I had seen many fathers do to their sons in junior golf), Dad simply said: "What can we learn from today? Let's look at the bright side. There are a lot of things we can pick out and work on so that you'll be better next time."

At the time, we had a little pickup truck with a camper top on it. During the long ride home, I rode in the back and climbed up near the window—and my dad and I talked for the entire ride home. We analyzed each shot and what I was thinking. He asked me where I went wrong and what I thought I could do to get better. He made suggestions. And together we talked about what to practice when I got home and how to play smarter in the next event.

After I started winning some of those junior golf tournaments, I announced to my dad that I wanted to play golf for a living. "Well, that's great, Philip," he said. "I just want you to realize how many people try to play on the PGA Tour—and how many actually make it. So let's make sure you go to college to set up some other options if that dream falls through."

Back then, playing professional golf was just that for me—a dream. It's all I wanted to do since I was about nine or ten.

———

I was in the kitchen cooking during Sunday's final round of the 1980 Masters Golf Tournament. Philip was in the living room watching television when, all of a sudden, he started yelling: "Mom! Mom! Come here! Come here!" I went in to see what was going on and there on the television was the leader of the tournament (Seve Ballesteros) walking up the fairway to the 18th green. People were cheering for him and he was waving back.

"You see, Mom," said Philip, pointing to the television, "one day that's going to be me—and they're going to be clapping and yelling for me! I'm going to win the Masters and be walking up to the 18th green just like that!"

Mary Mickelson

Off the green on #3, I decide to use my putter for this tricky little shot over the ridge. It's a prime example of one of the facets of my game that I've been working on in the off-season with my short-game coach, Dave Pelz. Two weeks before each major tournament, when nobody else was around, we'd go out to the courses and play all kinds of shots. And before the Masters, we had played here at Augusta National and practiced, among many others, this very shot with the exact same pin placement. So I know precisely what I need to do.

I'm about five yards off the green. I have to be careful because the blades of grass are leaning toward me. When the ball gets up on the green, I don't want it to be going too fast. All I want to do here is to stop the ball within my three-foot putting circle where I feel very comfortable.

In hitting the shot, I judge the speed well, but I hit it farther to the left than I want. It comes to rest about three and one-half feet from the hole—just outside my circle. The problem I have now, however, is that I've left myself a putt that is downhill, very fast, and breaks three or four inches to the right. I'll have to hit it tentatively or it will go five or six feet by. Then I'll be in worse shape.

This putt is for par. I start it outside the left edge, but it breaks across the hole, catches the lip of the cup and rolls about a foot past. Feeling disappointed, I tap in for a bogey. It's my first bogey in 34 holes.

Well, I missed the putt. It's not that big a deal. Let's go to the 4th hole. As I walk off the green, people are applauding. I give them a smile and nod.

PLAYER	SCORE	HOLE
Mickelson	−6	3
DiMarco	−6	3*
Langer	−5	4
Casey	−4	4
Choi	−3	5
Singh	−2	8
Els	−2	5
Price	−1	7
Couples	E	7
Harrington	E	6
Jacobson	E	5
Triplett	E	5

*(Chris also bogeyed the 3rd hole)

Flowering Crab Apple
Par 3
205 yards

*T*his hole is a long par three with a very large green. It has two greenside bunkers, one on the front right, the other along the left side. But the big factor on #4 is the wind—which has historically shown that it can turn around on you instantaneously and wreck your tee shot. Several years ago, I played for the wind to hurt my ball, and it actually helped. The cameraman behind the green hurt his neck trying to follow the ball as it flew over his head.

In years past, the pin has always been on the back right—a placement I have always struggled with. But today, the pin is down low just behind the bunker. And that makes #4 another potential birdie hole.

I'm hitting the ball well and I feel I can take a risk. If I go long, the second shot is not very hard to get close. The ball will just funnel right down the hill. If I come up short, it's not a difficult bunker shot. So I'm going to hit a six iron and go right at the pin. I have to draw this one (left to right for a left-handed golfer) because it's not quite enough club otherwise (a draw usually goes farther than a fade). I make a good swing and hit the ball well. It's going right on line. But it falls about an inch *short and rolls down into the bunker. As I walk off the tee, I shake my head, and turn to Bones.*

"Yesterday, the wind helped, today it hurt."

"You're on an upslope," he responded. "Let's get it up and down."

When we got up to the green, sure enough, the ball was sitting up nicely in the sand. This would not be a hard up and down at all. My short-game coach, Dave Pelz, has statistics to back up nearly everything he talks to me about—and he once told me that a golfer's average bunker shot is eight yards. I never really thought about it before he mentioned it. But now, every time I'm in a bunker, I pick a target that is between eight and ten yards away. In the off-season, I practiced this particular shot thousands of times. In fact, I use a special practice wedge now because I wore out the grooves in my regular wedge. And where I used to be 60th or 70th in sand play, I'm now in the top ten or fifteen—and I get up and down to save par much more frequently.

I spend a lot of time practicing my bunker shots for another very good reason. As your bunker play improves, so does your driving accuracy. That's because your bunker swing is very rhythmic in tempo. You're not trying to pound the ball all the time. You simply let your club do the work. Repetitive bunker play develops a certain rhythm and that rhythm carries over to your driver.

I learned a long time ago that a big part of golf lies in the rhythm of your swing. And, believe me, each club in your bag has a tempo of its very own.

When Philip was a junior in high school, I wanted him to learn about the fine arts so that he could carry on a conversation about something other than golf. So he took a course in music appreciation. Well, he came home one day, said he had a test the next morning, and asked me to quiz him.

I remember being so excited to be working with him on something other than golf. This particular test was on composers of classical music. So I gave him the title of a music piece and he leaned back and thought for a moment. Then he looked at me and said: "That's a nine-iron. That's Schubert."

I tried another one—and he said: "That's a wedge. That's Mozart!"

Philip had memorized the great classical composers by relating their music to the tempo of different golf club swings. And you know what? He didn't miss a beat. He got all the answers correct!

Mary Mickelson

Even dating back to grammar school, my mom and dad were a bit concerned that the only thing I seemed to be interested in was golf. Television, books, people—everything was about golf. I even did my sixth grade science project on which compression golf ball was the best to use for junior golfers. It was really cool! I wrote to Titleist and they donated 80-, 90-, and 100-compression balls for my project. I don't remember which one was the best—but I got to keep all those golf balls!

After school, when the other kids would go out and play, I'd either play golf with my dad or, when he was out of town, practice in my back yard. When I was actually in school, I studied enough to do pretty well. And overall, I think my teachers liked me.

Philip would say to all of his teachers: "You're my favorite teacher. You do such a great job explaining things so I can understand. Thank you." Then when we would go into parent-teacher conferences, each teacher would say to us: "You know, I don't mean to brag, but I seem to be his favorite teacher."

After a while, they caught on. And later, when Philip would go up and put his arm around one of them, they'd say: "Yeah, I know, Philip. I'm you're favorite teacher!"

Phil and Mary Mickelson

Two things I enjoyed other than golf were football and baseball. I played them both starting at about age four or five. Later, I became quarterback on the football team, but when I broke my arm, I stopped playing because I thought it would ultimately hurt my golf game. And I really, *really* loved baseball. I was a pitcher (I threw right-handed) and actually pitched a no-hitter. I didn't have blinding speed, but I was deceptive and good at fooling the batters.

One summer when I was 11 or 12, however, I had to make a choice. It was either going to be baseball or golf. I had made the local all-star baseball team, but that required a lot of practice and dedication during the summer months—the very time that all my junior tournaments started. I just felt like I had to do one or the other. It couldn't be both.

So I went to my dad and we had a conversation that eventually elevated to the level of professional sports. "If you wanted to play baseball or golf professionally, which would you have the better chance at making?" he asked. I wasn't sure of the answer, so I said I didn't know.

"Well, in baseball, everything being equal, they're going to select the player who can run the fastest," he said. And of course, I knew I was not the swiftest person on two feet. So I was at a disadvantage in baseball because of speed.

Dad went on to say something else that really caught my attention. "In baseball, you're going to be a number on somebody's team," he said. "Maybe you'll want to play baseball in San Diego, but you'll be forced to move and play where your team plays. So in baseball, you don't have as much control over your own destiny. In golf, however, you can play when and where you want to—because you are your own boss. The flip side of the coin is that, in golf, you won't be guaranteed a paycheck."

We talked quite awhile about this—and I remember it being a very adult conversation. And at the end, my dad said: "But this decision is all up to you. Whatever you choose will make no difference to your mother and me. What *will* make a difference is *how* you go about pursuing it. And there's no problem with you trying to be the very best at whatever you choose."

I listened, asked questions, and thought a lot about what my dad and I had talked about. And not long thereafter, I chose golf over baseball. "Well," said Dad, "then it's up to you to tell your coach that you won't be available for baseball this summer."

Once I had made that decision, the years following really saw a significant increase in my dedication to golf. I started playing in a lot of American Junior Golf Association (AJGA) tournaments, which were national in scope. I was able to afford the trips for two reasons. First, my mom got a job working as a marketing director in a retirement home to pick up some extra cash. And second, I was able to fly for free because of my dad's experience with a major airline. So I became quite acclimated with commercial flying— calling to see if the flights were on time, whether they were completely booked or not, and which routes were the best ones for me to take to get to my destination. I started flying to tournaments when I was about fifteen.

———————

One day, we were driving Philip to the airport so he could fly to an AJGA event. And he quietly said: "You know, if I could just have some new golf balls, I think I could do better."

So we stopped and bought him a dozen new golf balls— one box. He was so grateful, he thanked and thanked and thanked us.

Well when he got to the tournament, he ended up sharing a room with Dave Stockton, Jr. (son of the great professional golfer). Well, Dave apparently had a lot of golf balls and Philip kept saying to him: "Dave! You don't know how lucky you are. Look at all these wonderful balls."

And when Philip returned home, he kept telling us: "Mom, Dad, you wouldn't believe how many dozens and dozens of golf balls Dave had! He had an entire suitcase filled with them!"

Phil and Mary Mickelson

———————

In 1984, when I turned 14, I started working at an inexpensive semi-private golf course near downtown San Diego called Stardust. I drove the picker on the driving range and picked up golf balls. In addition to my wages, I also had free practice privileges. It was a great place because the range was lit up at night and I was able to practice when it was quiet. The range was also right by a practice green so I could work on my putting as well.

When I moved on to high school, I continued my job at Stardust. In fact, I spent more time than ever there when I got my driver's license. I didn't go to very many parties or dances in high school. When all my friends were going out on Friday nights, I'd be over at Stardust until ten or eleven o'clock. On Saturdays, I'd leave home at six o'clock in the morning so I could make the first tee time—and then I'd play another 18 holes in the afternoon. After that, I'd hang around and hit balls on the driving range. When I finally did get home, I'd go straight to bed because I'd have to get up early on Sunday and do the same thing all over again.

After a while, Phil started winning some of these out-of-state golf tournaments. It was at that time we started thinking: "Now it's national. Maybe he really can be successful at making a pro career for himself."

Then we started saying to him: "Philip, you have a special talent. But that doesn't make you better than anyone else. It's what you are inside that counts."

Phil and Mary Mickelson

Somewhere along the way, I picked up a book about Ben Hogan, one of the greatest golfers in history. I became fascinated with him, learned everything I could about his life and career, and I even imagined playing against him when I was chipping around in my back yard. Ben Hogan used to hit a minimum of 500 golf balls a day—otherwise he thought he was regressing. And when I was in high school, that's what I felt I needed to do, too.

Phil was not pushed as a youngster. Rather, he pulled our parents along in his desire to play golf. It's as if it was his destiny. Golf was going to be Phil's calling, and he knew it.

Tina Mickelson, Phil's Sister

Spending time on the golf course and spending time with my family sometimes conflicted. But my mom, especially, saw to it that family always came first. We still went on our family outings right up through high school. And if the truth is told, I really did enjoy the time we spent together.

On one vacation, we had rented a houseboat so we could fish and water ski during the day. At night, we'd play cards. And one night, I taught my little brother a very important lesson in poker playing. Tim was eight years old and I was about fifteen. But that didn't matter. We were still competitive in virtually everything we did together. The two of us had been playing for a while when he took a restroom break. While he was gone, I stacked the deck so that he'd draw a king-high straight flush and I'd draw a royal flush.

Of course, that would give me the highest possible hand. When he came back and I dealt out the cards, Tim got really, really excited. I guess eight-year-olds don't have the greatest poker faces in the world. Anyway, he bet all his pennies on that one hand—about five dollars total.

"I call," I said. "What do you have?"

He turned over his cards and said: "Straight flush! King high! Ha!"

"Well, that's unfortunate," I replied, laying down my cards. "I have a royal flush!"

To this day, I have not gotten that money back. Whenever I bring it up, Phil always says: "Brother, it's the best $5 tip I ever gave you!"

Tim Mickelson, Phil's Brother

There were also one or two times I got into trouble playing golf when I really should have been at a family gathering. The one I remember most vividly was Thanksgiving Day in 1985. All of our family lived in San Diego. And that year, they were all coming over to our house for dinner.

I woke up that morning and asked my mom if she'd mind if I went out to play golf. "Philip," she said, "you can't play golf today. It's Thanksgiving and everybody is coming over."

"But Mom," I replied, "this is the best day. Nobody will be out on the course."

"Philip," she said again, with a little more serious tone, "this is Thanksgiving. You have to be here!"

Well, I just couldn't stand it. So I sneaked out of the house and went next door. I hadn't yet turned 16 and only had my learner's permit. But my buddy Chris Peters (the same little boy who ran away from home with me when we were two) had just turned 16 and had his license. Chris didn't want to leave the house on Thanksgiving, either. But I offered him $5, he said "okay," and then he drove me over to Stardust. I didn't worry about a return trip because I knew who would be coming to get me.

All the family came over to the house. Grandparents, aunts, uncles, brother, sisters and their families—about twenty people or so. And we were cooking and getting things ready for the meal. Then it came time to sit down for the meal, but we couldn't find Philip.

"Oh, Philip! Time to eat." No answer.

We went upstairs and knocked on his bedroom door. "Philip, are you in there?" No answer. We opened the door and he wasn't in his bedroom. "Philip! Philip! Where is he?"

And then Philip's dad says: "Check and see if his golf clubs are in the garage." Well, of course, the golf clubs were gone.

So I called over to the Peterses' house next door because I knew Philip couldn't drive anywhere by himself. Chris answered the telephone and this is how the conversation went:

"Chris, this is Mrs. Mickelson next door. You know, we're ready to sit down to dinner and we can't find Philip. Could he be over there?"

"No, Mrs. Mickelson. He's not over here."

"Chris, do you know where he is?"

Silence on the phone.

"Chris, his golf clubs are missing. Do you think they might be with him?"

"Well, you know, Mrs. Mickelson, I, umm, errr, umm . . ."

"Chris, it's okay. We'll find him."

We called the Stardust golf course and asked if Philip was there. "Oh, yes, he's here," came the response from the manager on duty. "He just teed off a little while ago."

Now I was the one who was teed off! So we sat everybody down at the table and said to them: "We'll be right back!"

Philip's father and I then drove down to Stardust, checked with the starter, and asked what hole he might be on. "He's probably on #3 by now," came the reply. So we walked out to the third green.

Philip was in the fairway when he saw us coming. He put his golf club back in his bag. Then he started shaking hands with the other three guys in his foursome and began walking toward us. We all walked over to the car and drove back to the house. Nobody said a word the entire time.

Finally, as we were pulling into the driveway, I turned around and looked at him. "Philip," I said, "there are some things that are more important than golf. This is family and we have to be here for this."

"Yes, I understand," he said. "From my point of view, how-ever—as Ben Hogan says: 'Every day that you don't practice is one day longer before you achieve greatness.'"

That struck a chord with me—and Phil did not get punished.

Mary Mickelson

———

As I step into the bunker on #4, I'm looking to see how far past the hole I can hit the ball. There's a little upslope there and I know it will roll back down. I know I have a huge margin of error. I'm going to try to hit the shot as soft as I can and fly it well over the front edge of the green so that I don't risk leaving it in the bunker. I have to keep in mind, how-ever, that the sand at Augusta is very inconsistent. Sometimes it is very heavy and I go right underneath it. On the other hand, sometimes it's very thin and it comes out too fast.

As I swing through this ball, I miss it slightly. It flies long, but still catches the slope, rolls right back down, and stops three feet from the hole—inside my circle. Even though it's a downhill putt, I haven't missed one of these all year. I'm very confident as I step up and knock it in for a par.

Chris DiMarco, however, bogeyed the hole—and now I have a one shot lead.

PLAYER	SCORE	HOLE
Mickelson	−6	4
DiMarco	−5	4
Langer	−4	4
Casey	−4	4
Choi	−3	5

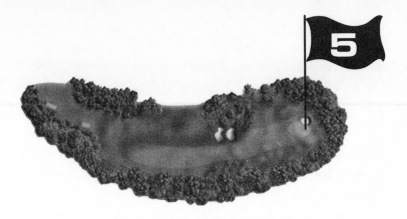

Magnolia
Par 4
455 yards
Dogleg Left

*T*he 5th at Augusta is a magnificent dogleg left with deep bunkers on the left side of the fairway at the turn. If I use a driver off the tee, I'll have to make a tentative swing to make certain I don't hit it in the bunkers—which are 315 yards out. So I take out a 3-wood because I can hit it as hard as I want and not be able to reach those bunkers. I make a good swing and hit it in the left side of the fairway— a good place to be.

For my second shot, I've got a good look at the large, sloping green. There is a back bunker that will catch balls if you hit it too hard. Earlier in the week, Tiger Woods missed the bunker to the right. His ball went down the hill, underneath the trees, and he wound up with an unplayable lie.

The pin on this green is back right near the bunker. I've got a 194-yard shot, so I pull out my 7-iron and decide to hit a hook (left to right for a left-handed golfer). I just want to get it on the green. If I go long, and hit it in the bunker, it's not that hard a shot to get up and down.

My swing feels very good, but the ball flies right into the back bunker. I really didn't want that to happen, but things could have been worse. If I'd aimed for the flag, my ball would have hit right on the down slope, kicked down to the trees, and I would have been looking at double bogey. As it is, I can still make par. I'm not concerned I missed this shot. It was a good miss.

Walking down the fairway, I glance over at Steve Loy, my friend and business manager. He grins at me and I know just what he's thinking: "Yeah, not what you wanted. But you've been in worse spots."

It was January 1991. I was a junior in college. On the 14th hole of the Tucson Open, I hit my drive into a deep gorge way right of the fairway. I was playing as an amateur in this PGA Tour event. Steve Loy was my college coach and caddying for me.

I remember standing next to Steve, looking down at that ball in what now looked like the deepest "canyon" I'd ever seen. We both agreed that there was no hope. I had to take a penalty drop. What made this shot so traumatic was that it was the final round on Sunday and I was leading the tournament by one shot.

On my next shot, I hit a 3-iron into another unplayable lie. Another penalty drop. Then I hit a wedge from 131 yards into a bunker behind the green. I blasted it out of the bunker and two putted for a triple bogey 8. All this on an easy par 5 that I could have birdied. As a result, I went from leading the tournament to trailing by two shots with four holes to go. Even though I parred the 15th and 17th holes and birdied the 16th, I found myself in the 18th fairway with a chance to win the tournament if I could make a birdie.

Phil hit his approach shot up on the green and left himself about a 10-foot putt. He was tied for the lead with Tom Purtzer. Now, remember, Phil was just an amateur, only twenty years old. I thought he was going to be scared to death when he went up there on the green. So I asked him if he wanted me to help him read the putt.

"No thanks, Coach," he replied. "I've got this. Just get out of the way."

And he stepped right up and sank that putt to win the Tucson Open. In doing so, he became one of the very few amateurs ever to win a PGA Tour event.

Coach Steve Loy, Phil's Business Manager

I don't specifically remember the first time I met Coach Loy. I think it was at a junior golf event somewhere. I do remember him introducing himself as the golf coach at Arkansas. But I was a Southern California boy and knew I was going to college somewhere in the southwest.

I specifically recall the first time I met Phil. I had just taken the job at Arkansas and was out scouting an AJGA event. I'd heard about this young 15-year-old golfing phenom who had just won his first national junior championship, and I wanted to meet him.

Phil was walking down the fairway with two cute girls on each side. They were all playing a practice round together. I positioned myself between them and their drives, and when they came walking by, I stepped up. "Hi, Phil," I said. "I'm Steve Loy, the new golf coach at the University of Arkansas."

He barely put his hand out as he was walking by, and he said, "Riiiiight."

I guess we both knew that was probably the last time I'd be talking to Phil Mickelson. He wasn't going to be moving from Southern California to Fayetteville, Arkansas.

Coach Steve Loy

Two years after I met him, Coach Loy accepted the position of golf coach at Arizona State University. At that time, I was a junior in high school and looking very closely at attending ASU for college. There were a number of things I liked about the university. First, it had great golf facilities—an 18-hole course with practice ranges that were right on campus. That meant that I would be able to go right from my morning classes to the course without having to take a 30-minute drive. Second, the weather was great in Tempe and I could play golf year round—just like in San Diego. And third, ASU was a good distance from home. Only a six hour drive, I felt I could go back when I wanted, but it was also far enough away that I felt like I was on my own.

Coach Loy sealed the deal for me. He spent time recruiting me, but he wasn't pushy in any way. I found him to be a guy who could not only be my coach, but my friend, as well. He had the intelligence and knowledge of the game to make me a better golfer. But

I did not feel that he was going to impose his personal swing me-chanics or game plan on me. I really thought that Coach Loy at Arizona State University was the right fit for me.

In college, Phil was a sensation. The cameras and the fans loved him. He had a rolled-up collar, a big smile, and was good looking. He was every mom's dream and every girl's hope.

In his four years at ASU, Phil tied Ben Crenshaw for most individual NCAA championship victories. As a team, we never finished out of the top three in the nation—and in his junior year, we won the national championship.

Phil's teammates called him either "The Roman," because he was invincible—or "The Franchise," because he meant so much to the team. Phil was a leader off the course as well as on. He led a good, clean, exemplary lifestyle. He was just a sensational kid.

Coach Steve Loy

When I played in the Tucson Open in 1991 during my junior year, the entire family showed up for all four days. My mom and dad, my sister, Tina, and my brother, Tim, were all there. I was also very fortunate to have Coach Loy with me as my caddy. It's not un-common for an amateur to have his coach caddy for him. Some people think it puts the golfer in an awkward spot—because the caddy really works for the golfer. But with Coach Loy, there was never any problem. In fact, he would tell me that I was the boss when we were on the course. I just think it was remarkable of him to be able to do that with no ego or insecurity problems.

During the third round on Saturday, I shot myself into contention with a 29 on the front side. When we came up to the 6th hole (short par 4), I pulled out my driver and drove the green as I'd done the previous two days. To drive it on the green was a risky shot, but I felt it was the right one to make. But I just hit that ball perfectly, knocked it right on the green, and had a putt for eagle.

Hal Sutton, Phil's playing partner that day, had laid up short of the trouble. As we were walking down the fairway to his ball, he leaned over to me and said: "You know, Coach, Phil really makes me mad. I'll sure be glad when he grows up and gets a little fear in his blood!"

Hal is a great friend of mine, and I laughed at his comment. But one thing I had learned about Phil over the years is that he always tries to hit the shot that can win—as opposed to the shot that will only keep the momentum going.

Coach Steve Loy

After I won the Tucson Open, things really changed for me. Before that tournament, not many people came out to watch me play. After that win, it was a good amount. All of a sudden, I was a professional prospect. But I can honesty tell you that I was not yet tempted to leave college and start the PGA Tour. Although there were a number of offers for a lot of cash to turn professional (as well as a few endorsement deals), I thought at the time that it was a shortsighted decision to leave college early. The amount of money I would earn in that last year and a half was nominal compared to what I could earn over the course of a full professional career.

A college degree is something that you cannot put a price tag on. I learned that at a young age from my parents. They instilled a belief in me that an education was very, very important. When I was growing up, it was never "will I go to college?"—it was "*where* will I go to college?" So I turned down all the offers and stayed at ASU. I know it was the right decision for me. And these days, when I'm asked to speak to young golfers, I always talk to them about the importance of staying in school and getting their educations. Consistent with our commitment to education, Amy and I formed a partnership with Exxon/Mobil in 2004 to create a national Math and Science Teacher's Academy based in the Washington, D.C., area.

I had a great time during that final year and a half of college. And I used the time, in part, to get ready for the PGA Tour. By winning the Tucson Open, I received a three-year exemption—which meant that I did not have to go through the grueling and competitive qualifying schools. I could simply declare myself a professional and enter most tournaments.

In preparation for turning pro, my family introduced me to Steve Taylor—a distant cousin who is independently wealthy and a financial genius. Steve gave me some of the best advice I've ever received—and I live by it to this day. He taught me to create a system of checks and balances—with a business manager, an independent money manager, and an accountant—who would all work together and answer to each other.

Steve also advised me to take half of my earnings right off the top and set up an account to pay taxes. The other half I should divide three ways. The first third I should place in low-risk, low-return investments. The second third, in high-risk, high-return investments. And the final third should be used for spending money. "What's the point of having money if you're not going have some fun and spend it?" said Steve.

He also recommended that I work on setting up partnerships with people—long-term relationships with those I trusted most. That was a recommendation that I had been thinking about anyway. And it led me right back to Coach Loy, because he was a great friend and I knew he cared about me. Rather than signing with a professional agency, I asked him to become my personal agent and business manager.

I was forty years old, had two children at home, and was doing very well in my career as a golf coach. But Phil is such a special guy that I determined it was time for me to make a career change. So when he turned pro, I went with him.

Coach Steve Loy

The next thing I had to do was find a caddy. I first met Jim Mackay while I was playing a practice round at the Tournament Players Championship in Jacksonville, Florida. Jim wrote me a nice handwritten note, short and to the point, that impressed me. So I called him up and we had a nice long conversation.

Jim had grown up in Florida, played co|
State University in Georgia, and had taken
But when an opportunity to caddy on the
he jumped at it. He'd caddied for both Larry
son since 1990. Somewhere along the wa|
named him "Bones" because he was so tall
name stuck.

After that one conversation, we decide|
pro, he would come along and we'd give w
That relationship really turned out to be a |
Bones has helped me in so many ways. He
golf inside and out, and is never, ever late t|
come good friends both on and off the cours
he married one of my future wife's best frien
the wedding was at our house.

─────────────────

Not long after I started caddying for Phil, |
between tournaments and we decided to g|
golf together. I didn't have my clubs with m
to have to rent some at the course. We drove
and when we arrived in the parking lot, I rea
a long walk (about 100 yards) to get to the
went around to the back, slung Phil's golf ba|
der, and started walking.

"Bones, wait a minute," said Phil. "What

"Well, I thought I'd carry your clubs up th
it, you know," I replied.

"No, no," he said. "Today's your day off. I'll carry my own
bs."

And he did carry his own clubs as we walked together up
the clubhouse. It was a small gesture that I will never for-
. And I think it says a lot about the kind of guy Phil Mick-
on really is.

Jim (Bones) Mackay, Phil's Caddy

———

in the bunker behind the #5 green. This shot is much harder
e one I had at #4. I'm concerned because I have to hit it very soft.
nker shot, the club never actually touches the ball. The sand is al-
between the two. My ball is on a bit of an upslope and I see an
nity to get the ball very close to the hole. So I open the face of the
y up. I'm going to hit a lob shot and just barely flip the ball onto
n.

ake a long, rhythmic, slightly aggressive swing—and my club
far underneath the ball. It doesn't get enough lift, hits the inside
the bunker, and falls back into the sand.

m disappointed in that miss, but there is no need to get down on
I'm often asked why I don't seem to get bothered by bad shots. My
is that I try to look at the long term. There's always going to be
n coming along the way. Everything will be okay. I've got another
ning. It's kind of a philosophy on life.

first thought after this shot is that I obviously went too far un-
h the ball because the sand is lighter than I had envisioned. I
level out my swing so that the club doesn't come into the ball so
d I go right underneath it again. I just want to get the next one
down.

I clean off the face of the club, look at the pin from behind the ball for a moment, and then step right up. I swing and plop the ball up about four feet from the hole—just outside my circle. Now I have a putt that will break to the left and is slightly downhill. Not a gimme by any means.

Now this is an important putt. I must make it to salvage a bogey. I make a good stroke and knock it in. As I walk off the green, I'm thinking: "Okay, I lost another shot to par. Those things happen. I'm going to make mistakes like that. But it's much better to make a bogey as opposed to a double bogey. At least I'm still tied for the lead."

PLAYER	SCORE	HOLE
Mickelson	−5	5
DiMarco	−5	5
Langer	−4	6
Casey	−3	5
Choi	−3	6
Singh	−3	9
Els	−2	6
Price	−1	7
Couples	−1	9
Love III	E	9
O'Meara	E	10

Juniper
Par 3
180 yards

*A*s I walk up to the tee box on #6, I'm thinking about my final round here in 1995 where I hit the ball long, made double bogey, and knocked myself right out the tournament. Today, the pin is in that same spot and I'll gladly take a par.

Chris DiMarco, using a six-iron, hits first and sends it long and into the crowd. He's right where I was in '95 and I know he's got trouble over there. I pull out an 8 iron in order to make certain I don't hit it too long. I want the ball to land just over the crest on the green—that'll give it twelve or thirteen yards in which to stop. The key here is that I've got to hit it far enough to catch the shelf—otherwise it'll roll way down to the left and off the green.

My swing feels good and the ball is going straight at the pin. It appears to hit on the shelf and I think it has stopped. But as I'm walking toward the green, I see the ball has just barely caught the slope, and is rolling back down the hill. It finally comes to rest a few yards off the green. From there, it's not nearly as hard a shot as being long would have been. I'm going to be chipping back up the hill and think I'll be able to stop it close.

As I walk down toward the green, I catch a glimpse of my wife, Amy, in the gallery. I know she's there supporting me. What a great feeling.

I first met Amy in the autumn of 1992 under somewhat unusual circumstances. Several of my golfing buddies and I went to a Guns N' Roses concert way out in West Phoenix. There was so much traffic that three of us left the car about two miles from the park and jogged through the desert to get to the concert site. (One of the guys stayed behind to drive the car up to the parking lot). We were jumping over ravines and sliding down slopes along with a lot of other people. We made it to the concert on time and, after it was over, hung out backstage awhile before going back to the car. As luck would have it, a huge rainstorm came up during the concert and really doused the area. It also caused a lot of flash flooding; in fact, a few cars in the low areas were actually washed away.

Due to all the flooding, a massive traffic jam out of the concert occurred. Nobody would be going anywhere for quite some time. So we pulled the car over and the four of us went to sleep. By sunrise the next morning, things had cleared up and we were able to get home by 7:30 a.m.

One of my buddies had been telling me for quite some time about this beautiful girl who lived upstairs in our apartment complex. "You've got to meet her," he kept saying. But I never took the time because I wasn't into going to parties and, besides, I was always too busy playing golf.

Well, when we pulled into the apartment complex, Amy McBride came bounding down the steps headed to her 7:40 morning class. She was dressed in shorts, a sweatshirt, and had a baseball cap on.

Boy, did she look awesome! I (on the other hand) had been up all night, was covered in mud, dirt, and dust—and must have smelled like a men's locker room.

My friend introduced us—and she was very nice. "Hi. How're you doing, Phil," she said. "Nice to meet you." She was so stunning that all I could say was "Hi." That's how I met my future wife—and it would never have happened if it hadn't been for that rainstorm the night before.

Two months later, I ran into Amy at a Special Olympics event during the Phoenix Open.

Part of my job with the Phoenix Suns was to work at the Phoenix Open hospitality tent. I didn't really like golf and wasn't feeling very well because I had just had my wisdom teeth pulled. So I tried to pay one of my co-workers to take my shift. But she had something else to do—so I had to go.

Sometimes, I think fate takes a hand in you meeting "the one"—because that's where Phil and I ran into each other for the second time.

Amy Mickelson, Phil's Wife

This time I didn't waste any time in asking Amy for a date. At first, she was reluctant to so much as give me her phone number. Actually, it took thirty minutes of persistent talking before she would even consider going out with me. Finally, she relented and we set up an afternoon date to play tennis a few days later.

I remember Amy calling me and saying she had a date with a guy she had just met. She said she was going on Saturday afternoon because it was easier to get out of a date during the day if it didn't work out.

I asked her what he was like and she responded: "He seems really shy and cute. But he's an athlete—and you know how those ASU athletes are."

Renee McBride, Amy's Mom

On our date, I found out that Amy had grown up in San Francisco and Salt Lake City, that she loved to dance, and that she was a member of the Phoenix Suns cheerleading and dance team. Actually, I was intrigued with just about everything Amy said and did. At twenty-one, the last thing I was looking for was a soul mate. But I knew right away that this girl was really something special.

The next day, I talked to Amy again and asked her how the date with the new guy went. She paused a moment and said: "You know, Mom, he is really a neat person—and so much fun. We laughed during the entire date. There's just something about this guy. I feel drawn to him."

I sensed a very different tone in my daughter's voice. And it wasn't long thereafter that I turned to her father and said: "Amy's going to marry this guy."

Renee McBride

When we first met, Amy was a junior at ASU. I had graduated and was just starting on the PGA Tour as a professional. Because I knew she was special, I wanted to introduce her to my world because it is not as glamorous as most people think. So I asked her to come to the 1993 Bob Hope Celebrity Pro Am in Palm Springs, California—which was only a few hours from Phoenix. "It'll be really fun," I told her.

When I first met Phil, I was only twenty years old and didn't know anything about golf. I grew up in a tennis family, and when he told me he was a pro golfer, I thought he worked in the shop at a golf course. I also thought that golfers were very nerdy and that it was a sport for old men. I could understand how golf would be challenging if they had big defenders coming at them like in football. But the ball just sits there on the ground. I mean, come on, how hard could it be?

Well, when he asked me to go to the Bob Hope tournament to see him, I thought we were going to be walking together on the golf course, holding hands and spending some fun time together.

Amy Mickelson

On Thursday, the day before Amy arrived, I played in the celebrity rotation with actor Joe Pesci, former football player and coach Mike Ditka, and another former football player, the *huge*

Lawrence Taylor. When we got to the 18th hole (which is a par 5 over water), Ditka hit a couple of shots in the water. Then Pesci hit a couple of shots in the water. And then Lawrence Taylor hit a couple of shots in the water. So my ball was the only one that counted when we got up to the green. At this point in the tournament, I was about even par (all the professionals' rounds count in the five-day event). So I was hoping to make the 15-foot birdie putt I had, not only to help our team, but also to get my own round going.

Well, I spent a lot of time lining up this putt. And it looked good from the moment I stroked it. The ball was rolling, rolling, rolling—going right on the line I thought it would. When it got about 18 inches from the hole, I started walking because I could tell the ball was going right in the middle of the cup.

Then all of a sudden, out of nowhere, another ball came rolling onto the green, hit my ball in mid-roll, and deflected it off its path—and I didn't make my birdie. I looked over in the direction where the ball came from and Lawrence Taylor was standing there with this sheepish look on his face. He had been practice putting and hit my ball.

"Sorry," he said.

Well, I was really hacked off and started walking toward him to give him a piece of my mind. But he got bigger and bigger as I got closer and closer—and all I could get out of my mouth was: "No problem, L.T." For gosh sakes, what else could I say to Lawrence Taylor? I got over it quickly, though, because Amy showed up for the next day's round of golf.

The Bob Hope Pro Am always has a fun atmosphere, which is why I thought it would be a great place for her to be introduced to pro golf. But I forget that there are a lot of pretty girls running around wearing T-shirts that say, "Bob Hope Classic." And the girls will sometimes walk inside the gallery ropes and flirt with the golfers and celebrities. When a few of them came up and started talking to me, I saw Amy out of the corner of my eye and could tell she was not happy.

———

To say that I was not happy is an understatement. I thought we were at least going to be spending some time together. That day, Phil only had about a dozen people following him, including me. The Bob Hope girls were inside the ropes giggling and flirting with Phil and his playing partner. I didn't know what was going on or who these girls were. I had rearranged my entire schedule to be able to see Phil. But now I was thinking that there were a lot of other nice boys in the world. I didn't need this.

Amy Mickelson

———

Well, this may not have been the smartest thing in the world to do, but I decided to play a joke on Amy. I wrote out a little note and wrapped it around my hotel room key. There were about a dozen people in the group following us. So I asked Bones to take the note to "that little blonde over there." And he said, "Sure thing."

———

Bones the caddy came over to me and said: "My boss told me to give this to you." And I thought, "Well, he's trying to make up with a nice little note. That's so sweet."

But I just didn't understand why he handed it to me because Phil was standing on the edge of the green (only ten feet away) with a big grin on his face. When I opened the note, the hotel room key fell onto the ground. And the ladies who were standing around me just gasped.

Well, I was so mad, I picked up the key and threw it at Phil as hard as I could.

Amy Mickelson

Luckily, Amy had a great sense of humor and, fortunately, forgave me for the prank. It wasn't long after the tournament that we started getting really close. A couple of months later, Amy visited me when I played in another tournament (the Western Open). I was paired with Justin Leonard (future British Open champion), who at that time was a young up and comer. Even back then, Justin was known for his consistent play. Solid in the fairways, great approaches to the greens, lots of birdie and par putts. He was just a terrific golfer, period. Amy followed along in the gallery with us. It was her very first professional golfing event—and I remember wondering what she was thinking at the time.

I really thought Justin was a very boring player. He *always* hit it in the fairway. He *always* hit it up there on the green. Then he'd hit one or two putts and he was done.

Phil, on the other hand, was having much more fun. He hardly ever hit it in the fairway. And he'd hit these shots that would bend around the trees. And when he was in the bunkers around the green (which was often), he'd hit the ball right up there next to the pin. It was fun to watch.

Amy Mickelson

That day, Justin and I were also playing with 1995 Masters champion Ben Crenshaw. Amy followed along for the entire round and I saw her spending a lot of time with Ben's wife. At dinner that night, Amy really seemed to have picked up a pretty good knowledge of golf.

Julie Crenshaw, Ben's wife, came up to me after one of the early holes, introduced herself, and said: "That was a great birdie Phil made."

"What's a birdie?" I asked.

Julie smiled at me and said, "What in the world do you and Phil talk about?"

"Not golf," I responded.

Well, Julie spent that entire round teaching me about birdies, eagles, bogeys, double bogeys, honors, par 3s, par 4s, and par 5s. On the back nine, she'd quiz me. "Okay, is this a par 4 or a par 5?" she would ask. Then when we'd go up to the next hole, she'd ask: "Okay, who has the honors?"

So in one round, thanks to Julie Crenshaw, I got a terrific golf education.

Amy Mickelson

It wasn't long before Amy and I were spending every moment we could together. I was new on the PGA Tour at the time and missed a lot of tournament cuts—which meant that I didn't get to play on Saturdays and Sundays. It wasn't good for my career, but Amy liked it when I missed cuts because I'd come home two days early.

We soon started to get very serious in our relationship and, of course, that entailed a visit to Utah to meet her parents. So six months after we met, Amy and I flew to Salt Lake City.

Okay, this was big. Really big. I told Mom and Dad that I wanted to marry this boy.

I was a mess. I was so nervous. I wanted them to love him as much as I did.

Amy Mickelson

During that first meeting with Amy's parents, I probably didn't show my very best colors. However, I did show my *true* colors because I wanted to make sure they knew I wasn't trying to sugarcoat anything. So I pretty much put myself out there.

That evening, we all came back to the house after a nice dinner and were sitting around watching *Cheers*, my favorite television show. I mentioned to everybody that the producers of *Cheers* had called me and asked me if I wanted to sit at the bar on one of the show's final episodes. But things just didn't work out because of my schedule.

"Man!" I said. "I would have given my *left nut* to have been on that show!"

I admit that might have not been the smartest thing to say out loud—and I regretted it the moment I said it. Amy's father and little brother thought it was really funny. But her mom kind of grimaced. After that, I figured I needed to do something to show her mom that I wasn't a complete moron.

Fairly early in their relationship, Amy and Phil were at our house and talking about their similarities. They were acting like they were meant to be together.

"We both have a *big sister*," they said. "And they both have blue eyes."

"We both have a *little brother*. And *they* both have *brown* eyes."

"We're both the *middle child*. And *we* both have *green* eyes."

They would just sit at the table and stare at each other.

Gary McBride, Amy's Dad

A couple of months later, I managed to endear myself to Amy's father, as well. I had this little event at Euro Disney in France and I asked her to go with me. "Hey, why don't we go to Paris together. It will be really fun. We'll go for a week and see the Eiffel Tower. What do you think?"

"Oh, I'd love to go," she responded, "but I really don't think my dad would let me."

"Come on," I said, "you're an adult."

"I don't think so."

"Tell you what, I'll call your father."

"No, that doesn't sound like such a good idea. Maybe I should call him."

We went back and forth for a week about who should call her father about this trip to Paris. So finally, I called him.

"Mr. McBride, I love your daughter," I said. "We really are in love—and I'm going to Paris and it would really be fun if she could go with me. There would be separate rooms, of course."

You know, that phone call kind of hit me wrong. Phil was nice, very nice. But dads are pretty protective of their daughters. And when he said they would have separate rooms, I was thinking: "Right—like there are no hallways."

Gary McBride

After thinking about it for a few seconds, my dad called me up. "Amy," he said, "if you marry Phil, there will be lots of trips. If you don't marry him, then you shouldn't be going on this particular trip. This is your decision, Amy. *But you're not going.*"

So I told Phil and he agreed with me that I shouldn't go to Paris with him.

But we've been married for quite some time now—and I still haven't been to Paris.

Amy Mickelson

That same year (1993), I won my first tournament as a professional. It was the Buick Open in my hometown of San Diego—and the first thing I did after I won was to call Amy—who was back at her apartment in Tempe. "Did you see me?" I asked. "I was on television. I just won my first tournament."

"No," she said. "I was down at the swimming pool with my girlfriends."

Because Amy was working for the NBA at the time, she figured that golf was much like basketball where you won fifty or more percent of your games. And she figured that golf was much the same. "Well, this is a really big thing, Amy," I said. "This is a huge day for me. I want you to come out to San Diego and celebrate with my family and me. It would mean a lot to me." So that night, Amy got on a plane, flew out, and met my parents for the first time (We stayed in separate rooms, of course.)

One of the things I did after I won the Buick Open was to present my grandfather (Alfred Santos, my mom's dad) a white flag from the tournament. He took it and proudly put it up on the wall of his kitchen. That was a tradition I established—he got a flag after every win.

My grandfather had a tough upbringing. He was forced to leave high school in order to help provide for his family. So he became a professional fisherman, which took him away from home for months at a time. But when he got married and had three daughters, he made a key decision. He sold his fishing business, took the money and invested it, and then started working small odd jobs here and there. In other words, he sacrificed his own prosperity to be home to help my grandmother raise my mom and her two sisters.

My grandfather put his family first but, with hard work and some shrewd investments, he still became a success. I always admired the fact that he was able to win at both and, in that respect, I've tried to model myself after him.

During my early years on the PGA Tour, I won a few and lost a few. But I always attempted to enjoy myself. The after-round press conferences would often get a little boring. The reporters would ask the same old questions. "Why did you use a six-iron on #8?" "Why did you go for the green and hit it in the water when you could have laid up?" Stuff like that. Well, at one of my early press conferences, I noticed this guy sitting in the front row who was furiously writing down almost every word I said. He rarely ever looked up at me. Eventually, he raised his hand to ask a question.

"Phil, word has it that you're a genius," he said. "Is that true?" "Well, it used to be true," I responded seriously. "But my parents wanted me to be normal. So they took me to a surgeon and he reversed my IQ so that I wouldn't be a genius."

This reporter was writing down every word as it came out of my mouth. Finally, he got this funny expression on his face, looked up at me, and said: "Really?"

"No, not really," I responded. "But I gotcha, didn't I?"

Phil used to visit me at ASU whenever he got the chance. One day, we were at a charity golf event and Phil met this little boy who could not catch very well.

So, in order to build up his confidence, Phil asked the boy to stand about three feet away and face in the opposite direction. "Now hold your hat straight out from your body and don't move."

Then Phil took a wedge and chipped the ball over the boy's head and it flew right into the hat. Phil went up and shook the boy's hand, gave him the ball, and said: "See, you *can* catch. Thank you. You've been a great assistant."

Well, that kid's eyes were as round as saucers. "Mister," he said, "you are a magician."

Amy Mickelson

For my second shot on #6, I've got about 90 feet to the hole. I don't think there's enough room to fly the ball high in the air and stop it close to the hole. So I decide to hit a basic chip and bump the ball into the hill. But it hits the hill a little bit too hard—and the ball rolls twelve feet past the hole. I overdid this one—it was not nearly as hard a shot as I'd originally thought.

Now I've got a testy putt that breaks left to right and will move quickly down the hill. I've got to make this for par. I make a good stroke, but slightly misjudge the break. My ball rolls three feet by the hole—just inside my circle. I quickly step up and knock it in.

As I walk off the green, I'm obviously not overly ecstatic. I'm thinking to myself: "Okay I just bogeyed #3, #5, and #6. Three bogeys in the last four holes. I'm two over for the day. This is not going the way I had hoped. But the first six holes at Augusta are pretty tough. And #7, #8, and #9 are birdie holes."

All of a sudden, I hear some people in the crowd shouting encouragement. "C'mon, Phil. Get it together!" "C'mon, Phil. We can make this happen! We can pull it off!" It's almost as if they *were competing in the tournament.*

But I know I must get it going. I'm now tied with two-time Masters champion Bernhard Langer—one shot ahead of Chris DiMarco (who had a tough double bogey).

PLAYER	SCORE	HOLE
Mickelson	−4	6
Langer	−4	6
DiMarco	−3	5
Casey	−3	6
Els	−3	7
Choi	−2	7
Singh	−2	10

Pampas
Par 4
410 yards

*T*his is a very interesting hole because, if you hit the fairway on your tee shot, you only have a wedge or easy 9-iron for your approach shot to the green. Then it's a birdie hole. But if you miss the fairway, then it's one of the toughest pars at Augusta. You're going to be under some trees, hitting to an elevated green surrounded by bunkers, and you simply will not be able to get the ball on the green. This is one of the most critical tee shots I'll hit today—a birdie hole that could quickly become a bogey hole. Over the course of an eighteen hole round, #7 has the most shot relevance—and the greatest difficulty from which to recover.

I have driven it well all week, so I pull out my driver and aim down the right side and hit a slight cut. The fairway slopes slightly to the right, so this should work nicely. And it does. I hit the ball perfectly—290 yards down the middle of the fairway.

Now I have only 120 yards for my approach shot. It's uphill all the way, so it'll play a bit longer than average. The pin is at the front of the green with three bunkers surrounding it. This is a very delicate shot and

I'd rather be long than short. So I'm going to try to hit it past the hole and put some backspin on it. If I can do that, I'll have a birdie putt that I've made many times in the past. It's a downhill putt, but at the hole it levels out. So the ball should not run too far past the hole.

I pull out my gap wedge, take a full swing, and make a good shot. The ball hits on the green past the hole and rolls back. Good. Now I have an easy 15-footer for birdie.

The very first tournament I played in 1994 was the Mercedes Championships (January in San Diego). I was playing very well and, in fact, was leading going into Sunday's final round. So I called Amy and told her that I had a really good feeling about tomorrow and asked her to come out again to share the moment together.

We had been dating for over a year at this point and Amy was determined to stay in school and get her degree, which I fully supported. To help cover the costs of school, she held down two jobs—one teaching dance lessons to children, the other dancing at the Phoenix Suns' games. Often, when I was on tour, she would dance at a game on Friday night, catch a red-eye flight to be with me on Saturday, and then fly back late Sunday so she could make her Monday morning classes. We both would do whatever we could just to be together.

Well, when I called Amy about coming out for the final round of the Mercedes Championship, she had a conflict. The Suns were playing in a big Sunday afternoon game to be televised nationally. She was supposed to dance and there was no way her boss would let her go.

My roommate was also on the dancing team and we cooked up this dumb scheme to get me out of going to the game. While she was telling our boss that I was deathly ill—that I couldn't even get out of bed—I was flying to San Diego to be with Phil and his family.

Phil did win the tournament, and the live television coverage showed me hugging him afterward. Well, it just so happened that one of the Suns' VPs was watching the golf tournament. He went up to my boss and told her that Phil had just won the Mercedes Championship, that he had seen me there, and wasn't that just wonderful.

And my boss said, "Oh, you must be mistaken. Amy is deathly sick. She's home in bed."

"No," he replied, "I just saw her on television with Phil. She's in San Diego."

Well, I got busted. And I learned my lesson quickly. My boss chewed into me pretty good and suspended me for five games without pay. I had to sit on the sidelines just so I could keep my job.

Amy Mickelson

After winning the Mercedes Championship, I took some time off to go skiing. Unfortunately, one week off turned into more than three months off because I fell and broke my leg on one of the ski runs. My femur actually snapped in half, and, during surgery, the doctors stuck a rod inside the bone so it would heal properly. As part of my therapy, I had to start walking the very next day. But I couldn't play golf because all the muscles needed time to heal. So I was on crutches for three weeks with nothing to do. I missed the Masters that year and, I tell you, it was really tough watching the tournament on television.

During my rehabilitation, I would go to the medical clinic and undergo physical therapy for about three hours. Afterward, I'd drive down to the airport and take flying lessons. With my dad being a pilot, I was always interested in learning to fly. It was a great challenge to get my pilot's license and it wasn't long before I was certified to fly small planes. In the evenings, after flying all day, I would watch videos to learn magic tricks (mostly with cards).

I really had a lot of fun during those three months. When I finally did get back to the tour, I was rejuvenated and enthusiastic—and it really helped my golf game. During that down time, I also learned some new things. And today, I can still fly airplanes (with an instrument rating and a CE500 type rating), I can still do magic tricks, and my leg is stronger because of all the therapy. I'm not suggesting that people break a leg every once in a while—but it really isn't hard to turn a negative into a positive if you set your mind to it.

Of course, Amy was the first person I thought of when I got my pilot's license. I couldn't wait to take her up for a spin.

Phil called me right after he got his license. "I need you to come over," he said. "I want you to be my first passenger." So

I drove over to the airport and squeezed into this tiny little back seat behind him. And we took off.

Amy Mickelson

I was so excited to have Amy with me—and I wanted to show her all that I had learned. So I flew that little Cessna 172 out into a remote area of North Scottsdale and performed a lazy 8. That's where you pull straight up to almost a stall, add a little rudder, and go directly into a dive. Then you come down, go back up, and kind of fly over to the other side. It's not really aerobatics because all pilots have to do this maneuver (along with many others) in order to get their licenses. Lazy 8s and all the other arcing maneuvers you do in a plane remind me of a round of golf. You make one circle on the front nine, loop back to the clubhouse, and then do the same thing on the back nine. It's very similar.

On my next lazy 8 for Amy, as we were headed down, I started spinning the plane so that we were spiraling toward the ground. As I pulled the stick and leveled out, I looked into the back seat to see if Amy was having a good time. But her head was plastered up against the back wall, her hands were dug into the armrests, and her eyes were as wide as saucers. In truth, she had this look of terror on her face. And I thought to myself, "Uh, oh! I may have overdone it just a little bit."

Oh, I was furious with him. And I was sick to my stomach, too. When we landed, I drove straight home and stayed in bed for the rest of the day. I can tell you one thing: It took quite awhile for me to get in a plane with him again.

Amy Mickelson

——————————

Two years later, Amy accepted my proposal of marriage. (Actually, I think it took her that long to forgive me for the plane ride!) Anyway, on November 16, 1996, I became the luckiest guy in the world when we were married at the Grand Wailea on the island of Maui in Hawaii. It was a wonderful wedding in a small chapel, with both our families. Not a day goes by that I don't think how fortunate I am to have Amy as my life partner.

——————————

When we were planning the wedding ceremony, Phil knew that I loved to dance, so he suggested that we surprise everybody and do a tango when it came our turn to dance. We took a couple of lessons, but Phil wasn't the most natural dancer in the world. You know, he was a big athlete with size 13 feet.

We bought a tape of the music (we used the tango music from the dance scene in the movie *Scent of a Woman*). Phil would listen to it while he was driving around in his car and visualize himself dancing. It was very similar to how he visualizes his golf swing when he's out on the golf course. He would think, "slow, slow, quick quick, slow."

When we did the tango at our wedding, Phil didn't miss a step. It was a perfect dance routine on his part—including a deep, romantic dip at the end. What a moment!

Amy Mickelson

Picking your life partner is a critical decision for an individual's personal happiness. And in the world of professional golf, choosing your caddy is just about as critical—because it can mean the difference between success and failure.

Jim (Bones) Mackay has a professional, optimistic attitude every day we're together. He is not only a great guy, he's also an important element to my success. He documents every shot I hit—how far the ball flew, what the temperature and wind conditions were, and so on. Of course, I consult with Bones a lot on club and shot selection. And there's a public perception out there (created largely by the media) that Bones is like a good angel sitting on my shoulder. I'm always aggressive and going for the pin. He's always the voice of reason telling me to play the safe shot. Bones really is a bit more conservative than I am, but I think that makes for a great mix.

One day we were having a conversation about the fact that I always make the final decision. Of course, he agreed with that—but he asked me if he could have one veto a year. I thought about it for a minute and said: "Yeah, you can have a veto. You can call me off without question. But only one time. And if you use your veto up early in the year, you don't get another one later."

Bones has used his veto, too. One year at English Turn in New

Orleans, I had knocked my ball in the right rough behind some trees—and there was a lake between us and the green. I told Bones that I was going to skip the ball across the water, bounce it up the bank, and roll it on the green. He said, "I'm using my veto." So I chipped it back out into the fairway and made par.

Another year we were at the British Open in Muirfield, Scotland. My ball was down in one of those bunkers and I couldn't stand straight up. So I had to kneel down and try to hit it out of there with a 6-iron. "What are you doing?" asked Bones.

"I'm going for the green," I said.

"What!? No, no. We're going to use a wedge and hit it back into the fairway. We'll make par, bogey at worst."

"No, Bones, I'm going to blast this ball onto the green. You just watch."

So Bones said: "No, Phil. I can't bear it. I'm going to use my veto."

And I said: "No, you're not. The veto is only good in the United States."

Well, sure enough, I caught the ball a little thin, left it in the bunker, and ended up having to make a 15-foot putt for double bogey. Maybe I should have listened to him.

Because Bones is right so often, I feel the need to vindicate myself by playing some practical jokes on him every now and then. One time, we were on Hilton Head at the Harbor Town golf course. Behind the tee box at #12, there's a statue of a 4-foot baby alligator—and it's the most realistic statue that you'll ever see. Well, I remembered it from the previous year, but Bones did not. So I started tossing some tees at it. Bones grew up in Florida and knows how dangerous alligators can be—even baby ones. "No, no, Phil," he said, "don't aggravate him."

"Oh, it'll be all right, Bones. It's just a little thing."

Then I started sneaking up on the alligator from behind and Bones cautioned me again. "Phil, I know those things are small, but you can't believe how strong they are. They're aggressive and very quick. Do not mess with it!"

"Bones, Bones, calm down," I said. "I can take this little guy." So I jumped on the alligator and started rolling around on the ground with it. "I've got him! I've got him!" I kept yelling. I thought Bones was going to have a heart attack, because he dropped my bag, clubs flew everywhere, and he dove in to save me.

One other prank I pulled on my caddy happened during the 1997 U.S. Open at Congressional Country Club. He had picked me up so that Amy could have our car—and when we arrived in the parking lot, the place was just packed with spectators moving toward the golf course. So Bones had to stop and wait. Well, one of the fans wasn't looking where he was going and bumped his knee against our car. He looked up at Bones and then just kept going. Well, after we parked the car, Bones took my golf bag over to the driving range. Then, when he wasn't looking, I went over to four police officers who were standing nearby. They smiled when they recognized me and I said: "Okay, guys, here's the deal. I want you to go over to my caddy and tell him that he needs to come with you because he's being arrested for felony hit and run—and that the guy he hit is also filing a civil lawsuit against him."

So the cops go over to Bones on the driving range, tell him all this—and Bones just turns ashen. "But I wasn't even moving!" he protested. "He ran into me!"

"I don't care, sir," said one of the officers. "All I know is that you hit this man with your car and then you sped away—and the victim is now pressing charges. So we have to arrest you."

"What?! What! But I'm in this tournament. I'm Phil Mickelson's caddy!"

"Mister, I don't care who you are, you're coming with us!"

Well, I let this go on for about five minutes and then I went over there. "What's going on, guys?" I asked.

"Don't worry about it, Phil," said Bones.

"Mr. Mickelson," said an officer, "we're arresting your man for felony hit and run."

"By all means," I responded. "I saw the whole thing and you should take him away right now!" I think that's where Bones caught on, because he started to breathe again.

As I size up this 15-foot putt for birdie on #7, my only concern is which way it will break. Year in and year out, depending on how they alter the greens, it seems to break different ways. One year, a little left. The next year, a little right. This would be a great opportunity to pick up one of the shots I've lost. I stroke the ball nice and soft. I play it to break right, but it just doesn't move as much as I think. It's close, but I miss the hole and the ball stops about a foot away. Another quick tap-in for par. I'm a little bit disappointed. These are the types of putts—the 15- or 20-footers—I need to make if I'm going to have a chance to win.

As I'm walking to the 8th tee, I hear a roar from the crowd. Somebody's done something. But who, I'm not completely sure. These roars are very well known at Augusta—especially on Sundays. It's part of the magic of the Masters. They echo through the valleys and hollows here. Some people say that the enduring echoes are from golfing greats of the past: Bobby Jones, San Snead, Ben Hogan, Byron Nelson, Jack Nicklaus, Tom Watson.

We began to hear them this week on Friday's second round. They started on the first hole, rose in tempo all during the day, and hit a mag-

nificent crescendo at the 18th green. That was the day Arnold Palmer played his final competitive round here at Augusta National. Fifty consecutive Masters. Four green jackets. A lifetime of memories. I was thrilled just to be on the course that day.

Arnold Palmer.

A name synonymous with golf. A great man. A legend whose presence will always be felt here at Augusta. No one has done more for golf than Arnie.

After the first round of the 1994 U.S. Open, I saw Arnold Palmer go into the volunteer tent and stay for over an hour to sign autographs. It turned out that Mr. Palmer was signing for the thousand or so people who were donating their time to keep the tournament running smoothly. And he had kind words for everybody. "I know that you're all not going to be able to see much golf this week," he said. "But we all appreciate everything you do to make this tournament a success. You are all doing a great job."

That really stuck with me. I just thought it was a classy thing to do. In the years since, I've tried to emulate Mr. Palmer by setting aside some time after every round to accommodate as many autograph requests as I can.

A few years earlier, when I played in my first Masters, I called Mr. Palmer and asked if he would play a practice round with me. Well, not only did he agree to do so, he set up a foursome that included Jack Nicklaus and Hale Irwin. Well, Arnie (I called him Arnie on the golf course) and I teamed up and took on Jack and Hale. On the 7th hole, Arnie rolled in a 12-foot putt for birdie. On the 8th, he made another 12-footer for birdie. And on the 9th hole he knocked in his third birdie in a row, this time from 15 feet. O

that day, I got a glimpse of the Arnold Palmer of old—the fire in his eyes, the competitive spirit, and the magic that brought him four green jackets. It was a terrific day. Arnie and I won our little contest with Jack and Hale. By the way, Arnie and Jack between them have won ten green jackets. And I kind of wanted one for myself.

When I reach the 8th tee box, I have to wait for a few minutes. That's when I learn that the roar I heard was Ernie Els making an eagle putt up on the green ahead of me. So in an instant, I go from one ahead to one behind.

PLAYER	SCORE	HOLE
Els	−5	8
Mickelson	−4	7
Langer	−3	7
Casey	−3	7
DiMarco	−2	7
Singh	−2	12
Choi	−2	7
Couples	−1	10
Triplett	−1	8
Love III	E	10

My birth announcement.
(Mary Mickelson)

INTRODUCING

THE
Mickelson
"4 TH" SOME

PHILIP ALFRED hurried to join the Mickelson "3" some on the first tee at Mercy Hospital for a 3:45 PM starting time on JUNE 16TH.

Using all of HIS 8 lb 13 oz in a powerful swing, PHILIP proudly equalled HIS height with a tee shot of 21 inches.

PHILIP'S first message: "Let's play golf at my new home in San Diego".

Winning my first putting contest and developing my great fashion sense at age 4.
(Mary Mickelson)

With my dad at 18 months.
(*Mary Mickelson*)

On a family ski trip.
(*Mary Mickelson*)

With my bride and my family on the happiest day of my life.
(*Rick Shimomura*)

Instrument training in a
King Air 90.
(Personal Photo)

No tournament win had a
bigger impact on me than
the 1991 Tucson Open
as an amateur.
(Steve Loy)

Hanging with the greats at Augusta.
(Howdy Giles)

Some people consider the U.S. Amateur a major championship.
(Arizona State University Media Relations)

Learning to putt Augusta's greens from the one who did it best: Ben Crenshaw.
(Julie Crenshaw)

Me with my family: Amy, Me, Amanda, my parents Mary and Phil, my sister Tina, my brother Tim, and my grandparents Jennie and Alfred Santos.
(Ken Randall)

The man I admire most: my dad.
(PGA of America)

Steve Loy is my agent, but he's
more like a best friend or brother.
(Arizona State University Media Relations)

The woman of my dreams.
(Meri Friedman)

Tango!
(Rick Shimomura)

I cherish every moment we have together.
(Personal Photo)

I feel blessed.
(Luci Dumas)

Amanda in Montana catching her first rainbow trout.
(Personal Photo)

Amanda learning to fly.
(Luci Dumas)

Sophia melting her daddy.
(Luci Dumas)

Sophia with all her magic.
(Luci Dumas)

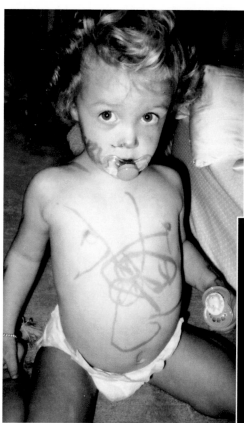

Sometimes Sophia acts like her mommy.
(Personal Photo)

A healthy Amy and Evan:
My mental picture of happiness.
(Luci Dumas)

Evan: A big
bundle of joy.
(Luci Dumas)

Obviously the President was wrong: I *can* dunk (with a little help from a trampoline at a Phoenix Suns game). *(NBA)*

Throwing batting practice to the Toledo Mud Hens. *(Golf Digest)*

Daddy the Knight, Amanda the Princess: Trick or Treat! *(Personal Photo)*

At a Tour wives' charity event: The PGA Tour Village People included, from left, me, Paul Azinger, Mark Calcavecchia, Payne Stewart, and Billy Mayfair. (*The Thunderbirds, image by Kay Eskridge*)

A moment I'll never forget: At the 1999 U.S. Open with Payne Stewart. (*AP*)

My grandfather and grandmother in their kitchen with the flags I've won. (*Joey Terrill / Golf Digest*)

Starting 2004 off right with a healthy family and a win at the Bob Hope.
(Darren Carroll/Golf Digest)

A little local support from the sky
at Torrey Pines.
(Getty)

My cutest caddy ever. Too bad it only lasted for one hole.
(Arizona State)

I couldn't ask for a better caddy or friend than Jim "Bones" Mackay.
(*Getty*)

This is what I look like when I'm
REALLY happy.
(*Getty*)

This is what Bones looks like when he's
REALLY happy.
(*AP*)

Amanda . . . Daddy won!
(*Golf Digest*)

The President roughing me up on my jump.
(*Augusta National*)

I can't imagine winning my first major without my friends and family
there to share it.
(*Augusta National and Barry Koenig*)

From one lefty—2003 Masters champion Mike Weir—to another.
(*Getty*)

ny approach, I absolutely do not want to be left of the green. I've
n there many times before and I've almost never been able to
and down for birdie. So I'm going to make sure that if I miss this
I'm going to miss it to the right side of the green and have a high
ty of an up and down.

I don't hit a particularly good second shot. And it does, in fact,
twenty yards right of the green. It may sound like I'm playing
ively at this point. But I really don't look at it that way. I'm try-
ptimize my chances of making a birdie. By being right of the
know I'm going to make par at worst—and birdie is a very real
y.

this course, I've got to put my ball in a spot where I can get it up
n. I simply cannot fire at every pin—because I can't hit a per-
every time. I have to cut my risk so that, when I miss a shot, it
do as much harm. In other words, in order to win the Masters,
to miss my way around Augusta.

out missing shots. In 1998, Amy and I were trying to get
nt but weren't being very successful. We consulted her doc-
were told that we might have to start looking into taking
treatments. Well, that was a big step, so while we were
g about it, we flew to Hawaii to attend the wedding of our
iends Rick and Tricia Smith. It was October 1998, and they
tting married in the same little chapel where we had taken
ws two years earlier.

the hotel, a staff member was telling us (and a number of
oung couples) about the mysticism and magic of the local
an Gods. He went over to a statue and said: "This is the
an God of Fertility. If you rub it, you are sure to conceive."

Amy and I at our post-victory party: We smiled this big for months.
(Tricia Smith)

Tricia Smith, Rick's wife and a vegetarian, making good on her promise
to eat beef if I won the Masters.
(Tricia Smith)

My post-Masters media tour was wild. Highlights included ringing the bell at the New York Stock Exchange, Leno, and Letterman.
(top: NY Stock Exchange; middle: NBC Studios, Inc., Paul Drinkwater/NBC Universal; bottom: ©CBS Broadcasting, Inc.)

Yellow Jasmine
Par 5
570 yards

*T*he 8th hole at Augusta is a long, beaut... initially grab my driver thinking I'm goin... so as to have an easier shot to make the ... have some second thoughts. First of all, I'm one... really want to make birdie. Second, the fairway ... the bunkers out there angle in to the left. And th... my ball will end up in an awkward gap where I ... club for my second shot. I usually hit my 3 w... 3-iron 230 yards—which creates a 40-yard "pr... driver, I'll be in that gap.

So I ask Bones to switch out the driver for t... tle more accurate, I'll avoid the fairway bunke... should be the perfect distance for another 3-woo... a 3-wood/3-wood combination will get me to th... them both well.

I make a good swing off the tee. The ball sta... and fades a little bit to the left. I'm in the fairwa...

F...
been ...
get it ...
3-woo...
proba...

V...
go ab...
conse...
ing t...
green...
possi...

C...
and ...
fect s...
doesn...
I've g...

Talk...
preg...
tor a...
ferti...
thin...
goo...
wer...
our...

oth...
Hav...
Hav...

Of course, Amy and I jokingly rubbed it—and so did two other couples.

After the trip, we began serious discussions about fertility treatments. During that time, Amy wasn't feeling very good—she was sleeping all day and just wasn't herself. So we took her to the doctor and guess what? She was pregnant—and we traced it right back to Hawaii. We later found out that the other two couples were pregnant, too. It turns out that all of us had our babies within seven days of each other. We should have respected the magic of the God of Fertility.

One evening, not long after we learned we were going to be parents, I took Amy to a Kenny G concert. Kenny and I had become good friends over the years and he invited us backstage before the show started. While the warm-up act was going on, he and I started playing Ping-Pong—and we made a friendly wager. If he beat me, I'd have to say in a televised interview that "Kenny G is a better golfer than I am." However, if I won, Kenny would have to play "Happy Birthday" to my mother-in-law at his upcoming concert in Salt Lake City. I thought that would be a pretty good way to make amends to her considering our first meeting.

After I gave Kenny G a sound beating in the "pong" department, he sent Gary and Renee McBride ringside tickets to his Salt Lake City concert. And right in the middle of the show, Kenny walked over in front of Amy's parents, shined a spotlight on Renee, and surprised her by saying to the crowd: "Ladies and gentlemen, today is my good friend Renee McBride's birthday. And I'd like to play 'Happy Birthday' for her."

For the next three or four days, I was golden in my mother-in-law's eyes. But then she started getting calls from all of her friends who also happened to be at that concert. "Renee, I didn't know you were such good friends with Kenny G. Is there any chance you can get him to play at our fundraiser next month?" She tried to explain that Kenny was not a really a good friend of hers, but I don't think anyone believed her.

In 1999, Kenny G and I teamed up in the AT&T pro am at Pebble Beach and really played well together. (He plays golf much better than he plays Ping-Pong.) When we came to the 18th hole on Sunday, we were actually leading the tournament (one stroke ahead of Tiger Woods and his partner, Jerry Chang). All we had to do was par the hole to win. However, I was also in contention for the outright victory among the professionals—and I needed to make a birdie to tie Davis Love III for the lead.

The 18th hole at Pebble Beach is a par 5 right next to the Pacific Ocean. I hit a great shot down right in the middle of the fairway. Then, rather than lay up, I pulled out my driver and tried to get my ball as close to the green as I possibly could.

———

Most Tour players believe that if (on a par 5) they can't get the ball on the green with their second shot, they should lay up 100 yards from the green. Statistically speaking, the worst shot is the 40-yard shot. (I've measured this over quite a few years; twenty-seven golfers at 1,000 shots each.)

Not only are the Tour players worse from 40 yards than they are from 100 yards, but it's also the *average* golfer's biggest weakness. The reason is that when they make a full swing at 40 yards, the ball just goes too far. Most golfers don't have a half-swing.

But Phil Mickelson does not have that problem. In the entire history of golf, there has never been a player who has swung better from 100 yards than Phil does from 40 yards. Actually, he's better from 40 than he is from 100. So that's why I always advise him to go against the grain of most golfers—and, rather than lay up, try to get his second shot on a par 5 as close to the green as possible. Statistically, he'll have a better chance of getting it up and down.

Dave Pelz, Phil's Short-Game Coach

The flagstick on 18 was over to the right—and there was also a right-to-left wind blowing toward the ocean. That's a unique situation because usually, at Pebble Beach, the wind blows in from the water. My goal on this particular shot was to try and hit the ball into the bunker near the green. Well, I hit it too high and with a little fade. The wind caught it and pushed it off into the ocean. I made bogey, lost the tournament—and Kenny G and I dropped down into a tie for first place and shared the trophy with Tiger and Jerry.

Afterward, of course, the media had a field day with that shot. "Why did you go for it?" "Why didn't you lay up?" "What were you thinking?"

Later that year (1999), I was selected to play in the Ryder Cup—a professional match-play tournament held every two years that pits an American team against a European team. It turned out to be one of the biggest highlights in my golfing career. The event was held in Brookline, Massachusetts, and we had an exceptional team of golfers that included David Duval, Jim Furyk, Jeff Maggert, Tom

Lehman, Justin Leonard, Davis Love III, Mark O'Meara, Steve Pate, Payne Stewart, Hal Sutton, and Tiger Woods. The United States had lost the last two Ryder Cups and our squad was determined to get the Cup back this year.

Unfortunately for us, the Europeans started out like gang-busters and seized the lead on the first day. I played well, but lost both of my matches. I had missed two important putts and was feeling down, so I asked our captain, Ben Crenshaw, to keep me out of the lineup on Saturday morning. I needed some time to fix my putting. I worked hard in the morning, and that afternoon, I paired up with Tom Lehman. We won that match to gain some much-needed confidence for the upcoming singles events.

Going into Sunday's final round, the Europeans still had a big lead (10-6). The night before, Ben Crenshaw pulled us all together and gave an emotional and inspiring speech. Then he told us that we were going to load up the top of the lineup and send our opponents a message. Tiger led off and won his match. I started third and won my match. Then we stayed on the sidelines and cheered on our teammates. And in what turned out to be one of the most dramatic finishes in Ryder Cup history, our American team came back to win it. The clinching shot came when Justin Leonard knocked in a 45-foot putt on #17 to secure a tie with Jose Maria Olázàbal. The half-point he earned gave our team $14\frac{1}{2}$ points— just enough to take the victory. (Amy's view of Justin Leonard's game has now changed from boring to *very* exciting.)

Afterwards, we all went up to the roof of the clubhouse and celebrated. I'll never forget looking out at the thousands of cheering people who had gathered around us. They extended 150 yards back down the 18th fairway. What an amazing moment! I was so proud to be a part of that team.

As great as playing in the Ryder Cup was for me, I'll always remember the year 1999 for a much more important event—the birth of our first child, Amanda. In an unusual twist of fate, her birth coincided with a major golf tournament, the United States Open in Pinehurst, North Carolina.

According to Amy's doctors, the delivery date was actually supposed to be a couple of weeks after the Open. But we weren't going to take any chances. I definitely wanted to be there with my wife when Amanda came into the world. So before I flew to Pinehurst, we discussed our options in quite a bit of detail.

We figured that the worst possible scenario was that I would go into labor on Saturday night while he was leading the tournament. Because if that happened, there were no ifs, ands, or buts about it—Phil was going to fly straight home. Of course, that would cause him to miss an opportunity to win his first major. But he told me over and over again, "If you have this baby without me, I'll never forgive you." And he made me promise to call him the moment I went into labor.

Amy Mickelson

We waited until Wednesday morning and went to the doctor for one final check. He stated that the worst-case scenario was unlikely to happen and that I should go to North Carolina and do my best. Amy agreed to be checked by her doctor every morning at eight o'clock. "Everything will be all right, honey," she said.

Before I left, I kissed her and said: "I'm going to win the U.S. Open, come straight home to you, and we're going to have our first baby together. It'll be the best week of our lives."

Very quickly, I made it clear to both the media and U.S. Open officials that, if my wife went into labor, I was going to leave. "Come on, Phil," one of the reporters said, "this is the U.S. Open—America's national championship of golf. You're not going to walk off the course if you're leading."

"I don't understand that thought process," I replied. "What in life is more important than your children?"

I played very well in the first three rounds of the tournament. Bones carried a pager in case Amy beeped us. We also had a mobile phone in my golf bag, but kept it turned off so the ringing wouldn't disturb anybody. One beep from Amy, however, and I would be calling her as I prepared to walk off the course.

After Saturday's round, I was trailing the tournament leader, Payne Stewart, by only one shot. We would be playing together in Sunday's final pairing.

I felt my first contraction on Thursday morning. "Oh, my gosh!" said our doctor. "If you had looked like this yesterday, there's no way I would have let Phil go to North Carolina."

By Saturday, the contractions were only four minutes apart. My mom and brother were timing them. "This can't be happening," I cried. "What are the chances? Should I page Phil? What if the baby doesn't come? He has a chance to win the U.S. Open! What are we going to do?"

I got so frantic at one point that my mom just grabbed me. "You need to get hold of yourself, Amy," she said. "If you don't, this baby is going to come."

We headed to the hospital and when the doctor walked in I begged him to give me Tribulatin, a drug that slows the labor process. "I just need twenty-four hours," I said. "Please!" Luckily, after a few hours, my contractions began to taper off. When they released me from the hospital, one of the nurses said: "Honey, I bet we're going to see you again in a few hours. This happens a lot. You're going to have this baby tonight."

I asked my brother to tape my knees together. "Just don't let the baby come for one more day," I said.

I never did call Phil.

Amy Mickelson

Sunday morning broke clear and sunny. It was Father's Day.

The first thing I did before I went to the golf course was call Amy. I asked her how she was feeling and she started to cry. "Why are you crying, sweetheart?" I asked.

"Just because I love you so much," she said. "Have fun today and win Amanda her first trophy."

I really was feeling good that day. I figured if I could just shoot 70, I could probably win. Twice during the round, I had a one-shot lead. But Payne would not back off. On the sixteenth hole, I missed the green on my second shot, made a bogey, and dropped back into a tie. Payne then stepped up and sank a great 40-foot putt to save par.

I was at home lying diagonally on the couch with four pillows under my lower body and a plate of Saltines resting on my belly. I was glued to the golf tournament—even though my doctor suggested I not watch because he thought too much emotion might start the labor contractions again. I was still on Tribulatin and the doctor had also given me a tranquilizer.

Amy Mickelson

Payne birdied #17 to take a one-shot lead and I missed an easy 8-footer for birdie that would have kept pace with him. So as we went to the final hole, I was a shot back. I played #18 well and made a solid par (for that total of 70 I'd hoped for). But Payne sank a 15-foot putt for par to win the tournament. Of course, he was ecstatic and went over and jumped into his caddy's arms. When I went up to congratulate him, Payne shook my hand and said: "I'm sorry, Phil. Congratulations on playing like a champion."

Then Payne cupped my face in his hands and said: "Phil, you're going to be a father and there's nothing greater in the world. You and Amy are going to make wonderful parents." I was just so impressed that Payne would be thinking about the situation Amy and I were in—let alone mentioning it on the green right after he had just won the U.S. Open.

As soon as I finished my post-round press conference, I flew home. When I arrived at the house, Amy and her mother were fast asleep and I didn't wake them up. It was a difficult night for me. That tournament meant a lot and I couldn't sleep. I kept thinking about the last few holes—reliving every shot. If only I had done this. If only I had done that. I finally fell asleep at 7:30 on Monday morning.

At 9:00 a.m., Amy's water broke and we rushed to the hospital. It's interesting to think about it now, but had Payne missed that 15-foot putt, I would have been teeing off with him in North Carolina for an 18-hole playoff to determine the winner of the 1999 U.S. Open—on that same Monday morning!

Amanda Brynn Mickelson was born on June 21, 1999, at 6:11 p.m.—just about twenty-four hours after the Open concluded. What magical timing. I simply cannot describe how special that feeling was when I saw my wife give birth to my daughter. There are few experiences in life that people always cherish—and those are the events we live for. For me, Amanda's birth was one of them. I never felt so at peace.

My friend Payne Stewart died later that year in a tragic airplane accident. It was Payne's destiny, I now believe, to have won the 1999 U.S. Open. But his passing just reinforces to me how inconsequential golf is in the larger game of life. Payne left behind his wife, Tracey, and their two children, Aaron and Chelsea. He was a very special person and I think of him often.

For my third shot on #8, I'm about twenty yards right of the green. All I have to do is pitch it over a mound and drop it behind the pin. Then the ball should catch a slight incline and roll back down to within five or six feet of the hole. So I hit a nice lob shot. The ball lands right where I wanted it to land. But it does not roll back down as far as I'd hoped. Now I have an interesting little ten-footer to make birdie. On the green, I really take a close look at this putt. Actually, it sets up per-

fectly for me. I love hooked putts like this—putts that move left to right. It's not downhill. It's not very quick. I can be aggressive and give it a good roll.

When Philip was in high school, he hit thousands of putts just like this one on the practice green at Stardust. And he hit most of them in the dark. After the sun went down, the green was poorly lit by a few small lights that were quite a distance away. He really couldn't see more than ten or fifteen feet. So he practiced those little left-to-right ten-footers over and over and over again.

Phil Mickelson, Sr., Phil's Dad

I'm confident as I stand over this putt. I make a very good stroke— and when the ball is about two or three feet from the hole, I think it's going right in the center of the cup. But during that last eight to ten inches, the ball stops its rate of turn, catches the left edge of the cup, and lips out. I breathe a deep, deep sigh because I'm so surprised the ball did not go in the hole. I quickly tap in for par. As we're walking off the green, I turn to Bones. "You're pager hasn't gone off, has it?"

"Nope, all clear," he responds. Bones' wife, Jen, is expecting their first child any day now. He's carrying a pager that is always on. We also have a phone in my bag, but it's turned off. Another major tournament. Another baby being born.

As we head for the 9th tee, I'm thinking that I just let two holes slip by (#7 and #8) on which I could have made birdie. I'm tied for second now, with Bernhard Langer and Paul Casey. We're all one shot behind Ernie Els.

PLAYER	SCORE	HOLE
Els	−5	9
Mickelson	−4	8
Langer	−4	8
Casey	−4	8
DiMarco	−3	8
Singh	−2	13
Garcia	−2	16
Choi	−1	10
Triplett	−1	10
Love III	E	12
Couples	E	12
Cink	E	10
Harrington	E	10
Price	E	10

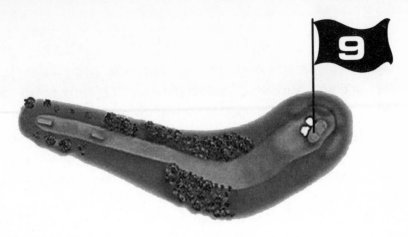

Carolina Cherry
Par 4
460 yards
Dogleg Left

*T*he front nine at Augusta rounds out with a superb closing hole. And it sets up well for me because of the dogleg left. So on the tee, I go ahead and rip a driver just like I've been doing all week— fading it to the left to take advantage of the dogleg. The ball lands just where I want it to—right in the center of the fairway.

Now I have 143 yards to the hole. My lie is on a downslope, but that's not going to be any problem. The green slopes from back to front, there are two bunkers on the left side, and the pin placement is toward the front. My goal here is to hit the ball close to the flag and stop it fast. But as I have been doing in most of this round so far, I fly it a little too far. My ball lands on the backside of the green leaving me a long putt. I don't think it'll be too bad from there. A par for sure, maybe birdie.

So I missed my second shot on the 9th hole at Augusta. But it was a good miss. Some people think I get lucky when I hit the ball too far and it still lands on the green. But I play them that way. There's no such thing as an impossible shot.

*   *   *

"Mr. and Mrs. Mickelson," said the doctor, "I'm sorry to tell you this, but it's all but impossible for you to conceive again. You are an infertile couple. It was almost a miracle that you had one baby. Mrs. Mickelson, you probably won't get pregnant again, but we'd like to explore some fertility options in order to give you a chance."

Amy and I agreed to undergo fertility treatments, but told the doctor that we'd begin after our one-week vacation to Hawaii. In January 2001, we went back to the Grand Wailea on Maui and again rubbed our hands on the Hawaiian God of Fertility. Six weeks later—Presto!—Amy was pregnant again. We never did start the fertility treatments. It's true. I swear. There must be magic in our lives.

All that year, while Amy was pregnant, I tried to spend as much time as possible with Amanda, who, at two, needed some attention. I remember one time when she was throwing one of those fits that all parents of kids her age have to go through. To try to get her to calm down, I let her watch a movie before bedtime. But she kept crying and complaining. This wasn't the movie she wanted. She wanted dessert and candy. She wanted this and that. So finally, I said: "Amanda, if you keep this up, we're not going to have a movie tonight." Well, she kept it up.

"I'm sorry, Amanda," I said, "but you chose to keep this up, so I have to turn off the movie." So I turned the movie off and put her in bed. Of course, now she really started screaming. "I want my movie! I want my movie!"

"Now, Amanda, we need to stop this. I'm going to leave the room and if I come back and you're still crying, the first thing that's going to go is your silkies" [her small baby blankets]." So I left and came back in a couple of minutes and she was still howling.

"Amanda," I said, "that's not a very good choice. So now I have to take away your silkies. I want you to know that if you keep yelling like this, the next thing to go will be your friends [her stuffed animals]. I don't want to take them away. I want you to sleep with your friends." I left again, but came back a few minutes later because she was still screaming.

"Amanda, it really makes me sad that you chose to lose your friends, too. Now you can cry here all you want. And tomorrow, if you can act better, you can have your silkies and your friends back. Then we'll start a new day." So I took Amanda's silkies and all ten of her stuffed animals and put them at the foot of our bed.

The next morning at about 7:30, she woke up and came into our room. "Daddy," she said sweetly, "I can act better today. Can I have my friends and silkies back now?"

"Yes, you can, Amanda," I said. And she embraced them all in her arms and took them back to her bed. And ever since then, Amanda always knows that when we say we're going to do something, we're really going to follow through. And it makes a big difference in how she behaves and reacts to us when she does something wrong. (That's a lesson learned from my parents coming around again with my own children).

Overall, I had a pretty good year in 2001, although I gained quite a bit of weight because Amy was pregnant. You know how it is—when she would eat, I would eat. When she didn't feel great, I didn't feel great. I think they call that "sympathy" pain.

I didn't feel any pain on the Tour, however. As a matter of fact, I was having a lot of fun. At the Bay Hill Invitational, I played a pretty good practical joke on Colin Montgomerie. Monty, of course, is from Great Britain. He has a wonderful sense of humor and he's one of those guys you can always joke around with.

While I was at the tournament, I read an article in the newspaper in which he was asked why he had not won any tournaments in the United States. He responded by saying that it was very difficult for him to play well because he always received very poor tee times. He said he was always teeing off either very early or very late. On the PGA Tour, of course, there are very strict rules for who tees off when. They always give midday tee times to those who have already won victories on the Tour to accommodate television. Those who have not won are assigned either early or late tee times.

Well, I thought Monty had made an interesting comment. So I asked a friend for a sheet of paper with an official PGA Tour letterhead and I wrote this short "official" note to Monty (which I left in his locker):

Dear Colin,

 After reading your comments in the newspaper, we at the PGA Tour Policy Board held an emergency meeting last night to discuss your concerns about these terrible tee times you've been receiving. We think we have a solution.

 Win a freaking tournament! [*Another G-rated version.*]
Sincerely,
The PGA Tour Policy Board

The next morning, I saw Monty out on the practice green. He would hit a few putts and then go over to his caddy and say: "I cannot believe they would send me such a letter!" Then he'd make a few more putts and go back to his caddy. "Can you imagine them doing that?" he'd say.

Well, after observing him for a few minutes, I grabbed my putter and a couple of golf balls and went over to the putting green. "Hi, Monty," I said. "Say, did you get my letter?"

"*You* did it?!" he shouted. "*You* did it?!"

On a more serious note, I almost managed to win the final major of 2001, the PGA Championship. That year it was held in Duluth, Georgia, and I really played well. I had three straight rounds of 66, but going into Sunday's last round, I was still trailing David Toms by two shots. David was really hot that week. He shot rounds of 66, 65, and 65—and on Saturday, he had a hole-in-one on the 15th hole only minutes after I had taken a two-shot lead with a birdie on the same hole.

During the final round on Sunday, I managed to catch David by chipping in from off the green for birdie. But when I went to the 16th tee, I was not in a patient frame of mind. I hit a tree with my drive, but the ball miraculously bounced back in the fairway. On my approach shot, I went right for the pin, but missed and left myself a 50-foot putt. Still impatient, I tried to make a spectacular putt to win the tournament but ended up running the ball eight feet past the cup. Then I missed that quick, downhill curling putt and made a bogey.

On the 18th green, David Toms sank a testy 10-footer for his par and won his first major championship by one shot. I'd had a great tournament and finished by myself in second place. And I was one of only three players in the field to shoot under par for all four days. One more time, however, I walked away without the trophy.

It didn't matter, though, because a few months later, Amy presented me with something far more valuable: our second daughter, Sophia. She was born on October 23, 2001, in the middle of the Tour Championship. This time, however, I took absolutely no chances and skipped the tournament completely. I didn't want Amy going through the same thing she'd experienced with Amanda, so I just stayed home.

Unlike Amanda, however, Sophia had some real problems after her birth. She had a cone head, she was purple, and her face seemed to be bleeding. Amy was fine, thank goodness, but we had to stay in the hospital for ten days with Sophia because of all her problems—which included jaundice, heart flutters, acid reflux, and colic.

After four or five days in the hospital, people would come to visit us and say, "Wow, Sophia is looking so much better. Her color is great and she's so much prettier."

Honestly, I didn't know what they were talking about. She was beautiful from the moment she came out.

Amy Mickelson

A day or so after Sophia was born, my mom and Amy's mom came over to the hospital to be with Amy, Amanda, and Sophia. The women sent me off to go see the Arizona Diamondbacks play in the World Series—a few hours' reprieve that I felt a bit reluctant to do, but they insisted.

Well, I was sitting in one of the first rows behind the Diamondbacks' dugout and the television camera apparently picked me up when they focused on right-handed batters. And sure enough, several members of the media blasted me. "If he can go to a baseball game, surely he can come play in a golf tournament.

But you know there's a big difference between three hours at a baseball game and six days away in another city. I bet there's not a mom in this country who'd fault me for my decision to stay home for the birth of our daughter.

Not long after Sophia got out of the hospital, I began taking up martial arts training. I learned very quickly that there is a lot of crossover application to golf. For instance, in your golf swing, you have to stabilize your lower body while you swing the club. And in the martial arts, you have to stabilize your hips when you make a kick. That training really helped me create better strength and balance for my golf swing. And I really loved the practice sessions.

Whatever Phil tries, he wants to be the best at it. He also wants to practice on everybody around him. When he was doing magic tricks, he was always asking people to "pick a card," and when he was into flying, he was always asking people to go fly with him. (Of course, I strongly advised anyone who would listen *not* to fly with Phil!)

Well, during this karate kick he was on, we were sharing an evening with several of our friends on Tour. After dinner was over, Phil went around to everyone saying: "Attack me! Strangle me!"

Most of the people looked at him like he was crazy—which, of course, he is. But Jeff Sluman's wife, Linda, said, "Okay, I'll attack you." And she leaped on his back and started pounding on him and clawing at him.

Oh, I was so embarrassed.

Amy Mickelson

In 2002, I finished second at the U.S. Open again. This time it was to Tiger Woods. The tournament was held up in New York at Bethpage, which is a public golf course. That seemed to make a big difference in the fan response. I mean the New Yorkers were great all week and really supported the event.

I started out kind of slow, but then began to make a lot of birdies on Saturday's third round. On Sunday, I played one group in front of Tiger, who had a five-shot lead over the field. He was really on fire during that entire tournament. I made a good run at him, but could only make up two of the five shots. Even though I finished second at another major, it was a very uplifting event for me. The people of New York gave me an experience I will always cherish.

I have to say that, by the end of 2002, I was really enjoying my career as a professional on the PGA Tour. With the exception of 1999, I had won at least one tournament every year. I had four victories each in 1996 and 2000, two victories each in 1993, 1997, 2001, and 2002, and one victory in the years 1994 and 1995.

So when I gave my grandfather his two flags for my victories in 2002, he looked up on his wall and counted them—twenty-one in all. Then he looked at me and said: "Philip, enough of these regular Tour wins. Don't bring me any more flags unless it's for a major. I want the Masters up there."

Back on the 9th green, I have a long putt—at least sixty feet. It has a big right to left break. I've had it before and I know it is not hard to get the ball close. I just have to get it to the tier about thirty feet away, and then let it slowly roll down to the cup. As I stand over the ball, I'm actually thinking I can hole it. The putt looks good from the moment I stroke it. But it misses by three or four inches just outside the left edge and rolls a foot by. I tap it in and walk off the green.

We've completed the front nine and have now circled back to the clubhouse. I have not shot a particularly good score, either. I'm out in 38 strokes—two over par. That's the bad news. The good news is that I'm still only one shot off the lead.

PLAYER	SCORE	HOLE
Els	−5	10
Mickelson	−4	9
Langer	−4	9
Garcia	−3	17
DiMarco	−3	9
Casey	−3	10
Singh	−2	14
Choi	−1	10

Camellia
Par 4
495 yards
Slight Dogleg Left

W alking over to the 10th tee, I turn to Chris DiMarco. He did not have a good front nine, either. But he's still only two shots off the lead.

"You know, Chris," I say, "for the last thirteen years, the winner of the Masters has come from the final pairing. Let's make sure it does for a fourteenth time."

"I agree," replies Chris.

This first hole on the back nine is traditionally the most difficult hole on the course. It's a very long par 4 with a treacherous green that slopes right to left. As I step up to the tee, I'm thinking that I definitely do not want to hook this drive. If I do, my ball will go through the fairway and off into the trees. So I want to make certain that I cut it right to left. Unfortunately, I over cut it by hanging on to the club during my swing—something I've done a number of times in the past. The ball goes way left. It clips some trees and lands in the edge of the woods. This is the first real mistake I've made today. Well, let's head up there and see what we've got.

As I'm walking, I'm thinking that I clearly had a bad front nine.

Now I've got to find a way to put it behind me so that I have a chance to win the Masters. But I've overcome adversity in the past and I can do it again.

The year 2003 was a particularly bad year for me and I had to find a way to put it behind me. For the first time since 1999, I didn't win a single tournament. In twenty-three starts, my highest finish was third at the Masters. I didn't finish in the top thirty on the money list. I went 0-5 in the President's Cup matches and let down my teammates. I had a terrible year driving off the tee—hitting very few fairways and seeming always to be in the rough. I was pathetic from 130 yards in—and before 2003, I was one of the best from that distance. I experimented with some mechanical things in my golf swing that didn't pan out. All in all, it was just a difficult year.

After the majors had been played, I really needed something to get my mind off golf. I started learning how to throw a baseball properly as part of my workout routine (to strengthen my rotator cuff and prevent injury). And when given the opportunity to spend three days with the Class AAA Toledo Mud Hens (a minor league baseball team in the Detroit Tigers organization), I took advantage of it.

I got to pitch and hit batting practice, field grounders and fly balls, and hang out with the professional baseball players. It made me feel like I was eleven years old again—back playing baseball in San Diego. It was just a lot of fun. It didn't seem to go over too well with the golf media, though. At any rate, it was just one more thing to deal with in a tough year.

I also made a dumb, off-hand comment about Tiger Woods

having inferior equipment—and it got twisted around to sound like the worst thing in the world. If you're in front of the camera every day for an extended period of time, you're bound to say stupid things you wish you could take back. So in an effort to end the controversy, I went in front of the cameras and essentially apologized to everybody. I believe Tiger and I have a good relationship and I felt bad that I might have said something that came across as disrespectful.

After all that happened in 2003, I was really feeling low. That's when Steve Taylor, my distant cousin and financial adviser, came over and had a heart-to-heart talk with me. Actually, he kind of slapped me in the face. "Listen, Phil," he said, "I want you to understand what's happening in your career and where it's heading. Right now, you are getting paid like a superstar, but you're not playing like one. So the first thing that'll happen is that you'll lose your sponsorships. And it will get worse from there. I'm not saying you need to play better. I'm not trying to put pressure on you. I'm just telling you the facts."

I thought a lot about that conversation. Many top athletes don't have anybody around who will tell them the truth. But here I was getting a good dose of the truth—and from a guy who manages my finances, but has never asked for anything or taken a dime from me.

Well, that slap in the face was just what I needed. It was time for me to make some changes—with both my attitude and the mechanics in my golf game.

The first thing I did was to consciously decide that I was going to put the entire year behind me. Don't think about it. Don't rehash it. Don't worry about it. Period. So I did not touch a golf club from mid-November until January 1, 2004.

The second thing I did was place a phone call to Rick Smith, my friend and long-game coach. "Rick," I said, "I need you to develop a game plan for me. You decide what I need to work on and how I need to achieve it.

Then I called Dave Pelz, my friend and short-game coach. "Dave, I need you to help me bring out my short game. I know I have the talent to be very effective from 150 yards, but I need you to develop a game plan on how to make it happen. What is it I need to practice? How do I practice? What do I do?"

Dave and I started working together right after the new year. He's one of the most interesting people I know. A former NASA scientist who worked on the first lunar landing, he eventually went out on his own because he loved golf so much. He started collecting all this scientific data from professional golfers—how they played certain holes, where to save strokes, where most strokes are lost. And over thirty years or so, he's accumulated a mountain of useful information—stuff that I just find absolutely fascinating. Let me give you an example.

Dave found out that the average margin of error is seven percent for a good player on the Tour. So a 200-yard shot will miss by fourteen yards either way. The very best ball-strikers on Tour have a five percent margin of error. So a 200-yard shot will miss by ten yards either way. See how it works? As a result, whenever I'm playing golf, I always keep in mind that the average margin of error is five to seven percent. If I have a 150-yard shot, I know I'm likely to miss it within either seven or eight yards to the right—or within seven or eight yards to the left. That's why I'm always talking about "missing" my way around golf courses—especially at Augusta National. In other words, I play like I'll probably miss a shot, but only by a certain small percentage.

Dave Pelz is also one of the world's foremost short-game experts. He specializes in chipping and putting. So we spent a great deal of time working on distance control around the greens and with short irons—especially wedges. With him coaching me, I hit thousands of golf balls and worked specifically on controlling the distance the ball flew and how much the ball spun after it landed. That practice really helped me improve and perfect my short game.

Phil has the ability to hit a wedge shot 132 yards rather than 137 yards. But it took years of training to be able to gain that skill. It's a combination of perfecting swing mechanics without fundamental errors—and developing proper club contact with the ball. Then, if you repeat it often enough, it gets committed to the subconscious. And when it all comes together, a proper shot results from a combined feeling in the hands, arms, and body.

The key is to get to the point where you're not thinking about it anymore; where it becomes like breathing; where you have a tremendously well-trained system that knows what it's going to do before it does it.

Dave Pelz, Phil's Short-Game Coach

Dave Pelz and I did a neat little trick a few years ago for the Golf Channel during the midst of all this practice. He stood three feet in front of me and I hit a flop shot over his head onto the green. The interesting thing about that is that Dave is 6'5" tall and the ball was above his head before it was even halfway to him. By the way, Pelz didn't even flinch when I swung the club! He's either fearless or overly trusting.

I also worked very hard on my long game with Rick Smith. One of the things we concentrated on was my driving—which was horrible in 2003 (I only hit 49 percent of the fairways). Rick and I have been working together since 1996, and he keeps track of every one of my golf swings. He went back and analyzed all that data in the computer and determined that I tended to get a little looser with my lower body when I was hitting the driver. In other words, I wasn't as stable. To fix that problem, I really started stepping up my martial arts work.

Rick also had me work on three main elements of my game. First, we focused on accuracy with the long clubs. I needed to do a better job of keeping the ball in play. So we throttled back a little bit on my aggressiveness with the driver and 3-wood. I stopped trying to slam the ball with a hook (which produces more distance) and started hitting a more controlled fade. Second, we worked very hard on distance control with my iron shots. I hit thousands and thousands of golf balls—and got to the point where I could predict within a couple of yards just how far the ball would go with each club.

It wasn't a matter of taming Phil's aggressiveness. It was a matter of creating a kind of "controlled aggression." Imagine competing against a guy who is consistent, accurate, and has incredible distance abilities—but one who can also get it up and down from the trees or never panic when he hits a bad shot. That combination is very hard to beat.

When you're working on long-distance shots, missing it a little bit to the left or a little bit to the right is not a big deal. But being short or long *is* a big deal. So, technically, we worked on distance accuracy with the long irons.

Rick Smith, Phil's Long-Game Coach

The third thing Rick and I worked on was taking the right side out of play. We actually worked on taking both sides out of play, but it's easier to make an aggressive swing and take out the right side. As a lefty, if I hit a hook, the ball comes off the face of the club faster because the face is squared-up and has less loft. It also has a faster ball speed. So when a hooked ball hits the ground, it's traveling at a lot faster speed. Therefore, it continues to run off line into further and deeper trouble. When I hit a fade, however, the face of the club opens up and adds loft. So the ball comes off the club a little slower, higher, and with less speed. And when it lands on the ground, it hits very softly and stops rolling. So my misses to the left are less likely to get me in trouble. To the right, the ball goes faster, farther, hotter, and continues going off line. That's why Rick and I worked so hard at taking the right side out of play—because my misses to the left don't get me in as much trouble. In business terms, I guess you could say that I was cutting my risk.

Of course, I'm not the first golfer to use this strategy. Jack Nicklaus, in his book *Golf My Way*, wrote that he would aim down the left edge of the fairway and hit a fade to the right. He would know the ball couldn't go left, so all he would have to worry about was not cutting the ball more than the width of the fairway. (Jack is a right-handed golfer, so he worked on taking the left side out of play; opposite from a lefty). Ben Hogan also did the same thing. And, of course, Jack Nicklaus and Ben Hogan were two of the very best drivers in the history of golf.

During this time, I also spent a great deal of time with my strength and conditioning coach, Sean Cochran—who used to work with the San Diego Padres. He helped me strengthen stabilizer muscles in my hips and legs, improve my overall core body strength, and increase my stamina.

I started on a regular exercise routine to enhance my cardiovascular condition. Mondays, Wednesdays, and Fridays: 30 minutes on cardiovascular work, core strength, and balance. Tuesdays, Thursdays, and Saturdays: 45 minutes of cardio, 20 minutes on flexibility, 30 minutes on martial arts.

And we changed my nutritional plan. No more simple sugars. No more buns for my *In-N-Out* cheeseburgers. No more doughnuts. More protein and complex carbohydrates. Rather than two or three big meals a day, I eat six small meals. That keeps my energy level running on high.

It all really worked, too. I lost fifteen pounds and got myself in the best physical condition of my life. So as the 2004 PGA Tour started to rev up, I was determined to put everything to good use. Dave Pelz's advice. Rick Smith's advice. Sean Cochran's training. My tighter swings. My new outlook. Everything.

Walking down the #10 fairway, I hear one of those tremendous roars coming from the 11th green. K. J. Choi has just holed his second shot from 220 yards out in the fairway for an incredible eagle. Is the Masters magic starting? Now I'm recalling that old saying: "The Masters doesn't start until the back nine on Sunday."

Okay, here we go! I'm only a shot back!

As I enter the edge of the woods, I see that my drive has left me under a tree. However, I'll still have a fairly open shot to the green. But when I come up on the ball, I notice that it's not only sitting on pine needles with a downhill lie, there is a pinecone resting against the front of my ball.

"Hey, Bones, look at this," I say. "We've got a pinecone in front of the ball." Bones looks at me and smiles.

"Wow," I'm thinking. "This is really cool."

When Philip was a teenager, he called me out into the back yard one day. He was standing in the bunker facing the neighbor's house. There was a golf ball on the upslope part of the bunker (in the grass)—and he was poised to hit it.

"Mom!" he said. "Watch this."

"Philip," I said, "you know the rule! You're not supposed to be aiming toward the neighbor's house!" Of course, he ignored me and swung anyway. Well, the ball flew back up over his shoulder and landed on the green behind him about a foot away from the flagstick.

"Philip, that's not funny!" I said.

But he just smiled and looked so proud of himself.

Mary Mickelson

When I got home from work, Philip showed me that backwards shot he had finally perfected. A lot of people limit themselves. They don't even think about doing something like that because it's out of bounds—or out of their frame of mind.

Over the years, Philip used his creative spark to dream up all kinds of crazy, out-of-the-ordinary shots. The tougher the shot, the neater he thought it was.

Phil Mickelson, Sr.

Some people would say that this is a risky shot. With a pinecone in front, you just don't know how the ball is going to come out. But I've hit so many shots with things in front of my ball that I know exactly how the ball is going to react. It's still a tough shot, but the pinecone being in front is not going to affect the flight of the ball at all. A pinecone behind the ball would be brutal because I would not be able to make solid contact. But in this case, the pinecone is in front of, and below the equator of the ball. Therefore, all the pinecone will do is compress the ball into its face. There will be no effect. My ball will go exactly where I want it to go. It'll be as if there was no pinecone there in the first place.

I take out a four iron and play a very similar shot to those I've hit all week. I aim at the bunker on the right side of the green and hit a slight fade. As I swing, the pinecone goes ten to fifteen yards down the fairway—and my ball stops right on the front fringe of the green. That was a good shot.

Okay, now I'm enjoying myself.

As I'm walking up to the green, I'm thinking I'll be able to putt this one close to the hole and at least make par. But it doesn't work out that way. I have a very large right to left break and the right side bunker extends into my line. So I can't putt the ball. I have to chip it. I pull out my wedge. I have a skinny, little lie (not a lot of grass under my ball)—so I can't get much spin on the ball to get it stopped. I hit the ball over the right edge of the bunker. But I hit it a touch too hard, it breaks ten to twelve inches, and runs about ten feet past the hole. I definitely would like for it to have been closer.

Now I have one of the biggest putts of the tournament. I simply must knock this one in to save par.

I hit a great putt. The ball just barely catches the right edge of the cup and falls in.

"All right!" I say.

Then I give it a little fist pump.

"Yes!"

All of us in the family have been here so many times that we stand in the same spots around each hole. And over the years, it just seems like something magical always happens on the back nine. At this point, Phil was very much still in it—but we just needed that little bit of magic. When he made that ten-foot par putt, my immediate reaction was: "Here we go!"

Amy Mickelson

That was a big putt for me. I did not give a shot back to the field. And the birdie holes are coming up.

PLAYER	SCORE	HOLE
Els	−5	11
Mickelson	−4	10
Langer	−4	10
Garcia	−3	18
DiMarco	−3	10
Choi	−3	12
Casey	−3	10
Singh	−2	15
Love III	−2	14
Couples	−2	14
Wittenberg (A)	E	17
Howell III	E	13
Price	E	13
Triplett	−1	12

White Dogwood
Par 4
490 yards
Dogleg Right

*T*his is the beginning of the famous "Amen Corner"—the treacherous three holes at Augusta (#11, #12, and #13) where one bad
gust of wind can unravel your entire round. The name was coined
in 1958 (the year Arnold Palmer won his first green jacket) by sports-
writer Herbert Warren Wind, who wrote that any golfer who could make
it safely through these holes should say a silent prayer of thanks.

The eleventh hole is also the site of Larry Mize's miraculous 140-foot
winning chip shot in 1987. He holed that shot in a sudden death playoff to beat Greg Norman and win his green jacket.

I tee my ball up on the far right side of the box because, as a slight
dogleg right, this hole sets up for a left to right draw. I hit a good drive,
but it doesn't draw as much as I want and the ball ends up catching the
first cut of grass 288 yards up on the left side of the fairway. It's not a big
deal, though. The ball seems to be sitting up fine and the pin is in the
back right of the green today.

When I get up there, however, I find I've got a tough approach shot.
There's a water hazard very close to the green on the left side. I have to

skirt the edge of the water within four or five yards—so there's not much margin for error. I'm 202 yards from the flag so I pull out a 6-iron with the thought of hitting a slight fade. This is a scary shot for me. I cannot miss it to the left because there is water over there, too. So I hit it directly at the pin and, for a moment, it looks like I'll have a very close birdie shot. I'm surprised, however, when the ball lands thirty feet short.

I'm on the green, though, with a good chance for birdie after safely avoiding the water.

One day, during a family trip to Montana, I took Amanda out fishing. We went to this lake that was well stocked with rainbow trout—so I knew she would catch some fish. We started out by throwing a couple of pieces of cheese in the water and the trout were there in seconds fighting for it. Overall, we caught about twenty and threw all but two back because the hooks were too deep to get out. "Okay, Amanda," I said, "we're going to cut the heads off of these two, gut them, and fry them up in the morning for breakfast."

"That's sounds like fun, Daddy."

So my daughter helped me cut off the heads, clean the fish, and put them in ziplock bags. At 5:00 o'clock the next morning, she woke up and came over to our bed. "Daddy! Daddy! Daddy! Let's get up and cook our rainbow trout!" So we got up, cooked the rainbow trout, and ate them for breakfast.

Little did I realize how big an impact that little outing made on Amanda. Four months later, she was sitting on Santa's lap. "What would you like for Christmas, Amanda?" asked Santa. "A doll?"

———

"No, I don't want a doll," I told Santa. "I want a rainbow trout. I'm going to cut its head off, gut it, and cook it for breakfast."

Amanda Mickelson, Phil's Daughter

———

So Santa Claus got Amanda a rainbow trout for Christmas. She and I cooked it up and ate it for breakfast. And for the next three Christmases, Amanda asked for a rainbow trout.

When Amy and I first became parents, we were very unsure of ourselves. So we collected a lot of information, made a lot of notes, and wrote down our questions about the best way to raise our daughter. Shortly after the birth, I was holding Amanda just outside the maternity room when Amy's doctor walked by. "I can't believe we're allowed to take home this *person* without any manual or instructions whatsoever," I said.

"Phil, you and Amy should just put your notes away," said the doctor. "You two are the parents. Whatever you decide is right." We thought that was an interesting piece of advice. And we've come to learn that there are, indeed, many different ways to raise children.

Both our moms and dads will take the children from time to time. And often, they will call us and ask how we handle certain situations with the kids. "We want to be consistent with the way *you* do it," they'll tell us. So Amy and I always know that our children won't be *completely* spoiled by their grandparents. That says a lot about our parents—not trying to force their ideas about parenting on us. But, rather, they're trying to learn and implement ours.

Of course, as we began to build a family of our own, Amy and

I were presented with what I thought would be something of a problem. I play somewhere around twenty-three PGA Tour events each season. That's means I'm on the road almost half the year. How were we going to keep the family together when I was traveling so much? Well, Amy solved that dilemma very fast. "We're coming with you," she said. And that's exactly what happens. I usually play about three events in a row and each time we leave, Amy packs luggage enough to fill three of those airport luggage carts. The current packing situation includes a double stroller, a single stroller, three car seats, a travel crib, a travel high chair, two bags of children's clothes, blankets, diapers, and one huge duffle bag full of toys (into which my golf clubs also fit very nicely).

Some people think I'm insane for taking our family out of town for every event. But I spoke with the PGA commissioner and he simply refused to put every tournament in San Diego—and I don't understand why!

My point, of course, is that some things are just not going to change. Phil's job is almost always out of town. And if we're going to be a family, this is what we feel we need to do.

Amy Mickelson

When we get to our destination, we have a set routine. Every Monday is family day. We'll take the kids and go to a museum, an amusement park, the local zoo, or whatever is in that city. Amanda especially likes museums with dinosaurs. She wants to be a paleontologist. (Did you know there are dinosaur museums all over the nation!) On Tuesdays, while I'm preparing for the tournament, Amy will find out what kinds of activities are happening for children in the area. And during the school year, she will coordinate with Amanda's (our two other children are not yet of school age) teachers back in San Diego.

I researched all the schools in our area and selected a very small, private one that had only two classrooms with seventeen children in each. That way, I knew Amanda wouldn't get lost in the shuffle.

I was very clear right from the beginning that I wanted our children to know their father and that Amanda would be traveling with us. And to their credit, the school officials and teachers were on board with us right from the very beginning.

We use the postal service, e-mail, and the telephone to keep Amanda hooked in with her classmates and schoolwork. Time is set aside each day for school, and our daughter never really misses anything that goes on. It's kind of a combination of home schooling and regular school.

Amanda will also pick one of our family's events to share with her class. When we were in Tampa, for example, we went on a dolphin cruise for kids. While there, we bought copies of an inexpensive book about dolphins and sent them back to the kids. And some of the moms called me and said: "My daughter got her little dolphin book and can't wait for Amanda to get back." We do a lot of little things like that to keep her connected to the kids in her school.

Amy Mickelson

───────────────────

Amy and I also try to make sure that the children are able to participate in all of the holidays and fun that every other kid gets to experience. On one Halloween, we had to be in Atlanta for the Tour Championship. Well, Amanda's costume party was scheduled for a Friday when I would be on the golf course. Amy made arrangements with the school so that Amanda could wear her Teenage Mutant Ninja Turtle outfit to class early in the week. And that worked out just fine. All the kids got to see how cool her costume was and Amanda just had the best time.

While we were in Atlanta, Amy also held a Halloween party at the hotel for the other kids who were there (including a really fun pumpkin-carving contest). And on Halloween night, Bones, Amy, and I took the kids trick-or-treating in a nice Atlanta neighborhood.

───────────────────

One of the reasons we're able to make all this work is that I know Phil will go to practice and play in the tournament and then he will come home and be with us.

I also admire the fact that Phil understands and appreciates the importance of family now—even though he's in the peak years of his profession. So when our children grow up, Phil won't look back and wish he had done anything different.

Of course, I also know that there is a lot of little kid in Phil, as well. He just loves being with our children.

Amy Mickelson

As much as I love being with the kids, I live for the moments Amy and I can share together, just the two of us. With that in mind, a friend of ours gave us an idea that really works well. Every year on our anniversary, we will take turns planning a special trip with each other in mind. I take the even years; Amy takes the odd. Every single detail is planned with the other person in mind. And on the off years, you just show up and get spoiled. One year, I'll put something together just for her. Then I'll surprise her with not only the destination, but all the events we'll do once we're there. She loves art history, so one year I planned a trip to Italy. Another time, she was pregnant and on bed rest, so I planned a quiet week at the hotel down the street. Then I filled the room with candles and arranged for an in-room pregnancy massage. The next year, she'll plan a trip for me. She knows I like more active things, so she has taken me skiing in Colorado as well as rafting and diving at the Great Barrier Reef in Australia.

It's a little tradition we have that gives us the chance to celebrate our anniversary—just the two of us, without the children, in an interesting location. We really look forward to it and I believe it helps our love for each other grow stronger as the years go by.

* * *

Up on the 11th green now, I do not have an overly difficult putt. It's thirty feet long and it breaks a decent amount from right to left. But it's all uphill, so I can be aggressive. I make a good stroke, but my ball falls off to the left and I leave it about a foot short. Then I quickly tap in for my par.

Even though I didn't make birdie, I'm still feeling confident. My game is turning around. I can feel it. Good things are going to happen. Let's go to #12.

PLAYER	SCORE	HOLE
Els	−5	11
Mickelson	−4	11
Langer	−4	12
Garcia	−3	18
DiMarco	−3	11
Couples	−3	16
Choi	−3	12
Casey	−2	12
Singh	−2	16
Love III	−2	16
Triplett	−1	13
Wittenberg (A)	E	18
Howell III	E	17
Goosen	E	17
Haas	E	15

Golden Bell
Par 3
155 yards

*T*he twelfth hole at Augusta is the shortest par 3 on the course—but one of the most dangerous, especially when the wind is blowing. Three bunkers surround the narrow green—one in front, two in back. And many a golf ball has rolled off the front of the green into Rae's Creek. Interestingly enough, the twelfth green is also the lowest point on the entire course.

#12 is a good example of why Augusta National is set up perfectly for a left-handed player. I've studied this hole carefully and analyzed the shot dispersion patterns for both right-handed and left-handed golfers. If a right-hander pulls his tee shot, he'll miss the pin long and to the left. If he slices it, he's going to miss it short and right. Either way, he's not going to be in a good position. Conversely, a lefty's shot dispersion pattern is going to be much more favorable. If I miss it short left, I'll be on the left front of the green. And if I miss it right, I'll be on the back right of the green. Therefore, as long as I don't completely blow the shot, I've got a pretty good chance to land on the green and have a birdie putt.

Just imagine hitting a thousand shots to the 12th green—and then letting all the balls lie there. That scatter would be your dispersion pattern.

A 20-handicap golfer would probably have 140 balls in the creek, 200 short of the creek, 150 in the azaleas behind the green, and then shots all over the place from left to right.

But Phil Mickelson's dispersion pattern would be very different. Out of 1,000 shots, he'd have 1 or 2 balls in the creek, 1 or 2 over the azaleas, a bunch of them left and right of the green, and a pile of them up around the pin.

Dave Pelz, Phil's Short-Game Coach

Today the pin has been placed on the right side of the green. I like that because one of the shots I've worked on all year is taking the right side out of play. With all those practice shots, I now know that there is something in my swing that will just not let the ball go to the right. It can only go left. And that's good because on this hole, if you miss it left, you can still make par. A miss to the right, however, and you've got trouble. You'll be in the water and looking at double bogey. So I have a lot of confidence as I walk up to the tee box.

When we got to the 12th hole on Friday's second round, Phil was about even par for the tournament. He was playing okay, but really hadn't yet gotten it going. But then he hit a great tee shot—only ten or twelve feet away—and made birdie. And he went on to birdie #13.

Jim (Bones) Mackay, Phil's Caddy

I grab my eight iron, stand behind the ball, and look out over the hole. I've decided to aim just right of the flag, take the right side out of play, and have the ball fall fractionally to the left. But just as I'm about ready to swing, I hear a huge roar coming from the direction of the 13th green. I think it might be Ernie Els taking another shot off par. [It was K. J. Choi making an extremely long putt for birdie. But I didn't know that at the time.]

I don't really pause. The roar just makes me more determined to be aggressive with this swing. I've been criticized by the media in the past because I've "gone for it" in key situations. But this time, it doesn't look like Ernie is coming back to the field. If I want to win the Masters, now is the time to take aim at the pin.

I look up at the green one more time and take my swing with a fairly low trajectory so as to neutralize any wind gusts. The ball starts right at the pin—I mean right at it. It moves about two yards left in the air and plops on the green only twelve feet from the flag. A beautiful shot.

The crowd around the tee gives a loud round of applause. I smile and nod to them. "Thank you," I say quietly as Bones and I walk down toward the green.

After Phil hit that great tee shot, I was excited. "Okay, Boss," I said, "this is the hole that got our tournament going on Friday.

This is the hole that is going to get our day going today. This is where it starts." And he replied: "Let's do it." But he also had this look in his eye—and I've seen that look before. It was the look that says, "Yeah, baby, I'm going to make this putt!"

Jim (Bones) Mackay

One of the great traditions on #12 is that after you hit your tee shot, you get to walk across Rae's Creek on the stone bridge named for golfing legend Ben Hogan.

Every day you don't practice is one day longer before you achieve greatness.

Ben Hogan

Well, I'm about halfway across the Ben Hogan Bridge when I hear this huge roar—again coming from the 13th green. This is my twelfth time at the Masters and I know the difference between a birdie roar and an eagle roar. And that was definitely an eagle roar. I figured it must have been Ernie Els—and, sure enough, it was. One of the television announcers described Ernie's eagle (which now gave him a three-shot lead) as "a dagger to [Phil Mickelson's] heart."

Well, I am not feeling any chest pains at the moment. Do you want to know what I'm thinking as I walk across the bridge? I'm thinking if I *can make this putt on #12 and then birdie #13, I'll only be one shot back with five holes to go. That's what I'm thinking.*

Before I head up to the green, I notice my mom. She's standing all by herself like she usually does. But she can't bear to watch while I'm putting. She'll close her eyes and say a prayer. I think that's interesting— my mom saying a prayer in the middle of Amen Corner.

For as far back as I can remember, my mom's parents always had their grandchildren over for dinner a few days after Christmas. My grandparents were the leaders of our clan. And every year on that evening, my grandfather would talk to each of us individually, tell us what he thought about each one of us. When Christmas 2003 rolled around, he was 97 years old, in failing health, and going downhill fast. He'd sleep almost all day and wake up only once in a while.

The grandchildren's dinner had been scheduled well over a month in advance—for December 28. That morning, he woke up early, fixed his own breakfast, and was busy throughout the day. In the evening, all the grandchildren came over for dinner—Tina, Tim, me, and all of our cousins were there. After eating, we all went into the living room and sat in a circle by the fireplace.

Usually, my grandfather and grandmother did most of the talking. But this year, because we knew it was going to be his last Christmas with us, we all decided to tell him what we thought of him and how much he meant to us. So we went around the room, one by one, and said some very special, private things. When it came around to me, I cried as I talked about all my fond memories of him—fishing together on the Kern River, playing golf together at Balboa, and all the wonderful stories he used to tell me about his own youth.

After we had all taken our turn, we could tell he was moved and appreciative of what we'd said to him. Then it was his turn to speak. He made a few private comments and then concluded with his favorite adage: "Always remember," he said. "You never cheat. You never lie. And the most important thing is your family. You help each other. And you stay close to each other. Always."

As we were all getting up to leave, my grandfather motioned for me to come over. "Philip," he said in a whisper, "this is your year. You're going to win the Masters."

That's the last thing he ever said to me. The next day, he told my mom: "Okay, I can go now." And he passed away ten days later—on January 8, 2004.

I have a framed picture of my grandfather and me together. It's on the nightstand by my bed. I see it every night.

As I'm walking around the green to size up this putt, I realize it's the exact same putt I've had on #12 for the last two years. The first year, I didn't play enough break and missed it low to the right. The second year, I played enough break, but I hit it too hard and missed it high to the left. As I step up to the ball and prepare to stroke it, I'm thinking that I have to play just the right amount of break and let it slowly fall into the cup.

Usually when Philip putts, I close my eyes and think back to when he was a youngster—and then wait for the crowd to tell me if he makes the putt or not. But as he was getting ready to putt on #12, I was thinking that Ernie was now three shots ahead and that Philip would have to birdie three holes just to catch him. Maybe it isn't going to happen today. So I closed my eyes and talked to my dad. "Dad, you told him he was going to win the Masters. What happened? Why are you letting him down? What's happening?"

Mary Mickelson, Phil's Mom

I start this ball out about eight to ten inches left of the hole. Then it starts turning, turning, turning to the right. And . . . the . . . ball . . . goes . . . right . . . into . . . the . . . hole. Birdie! It took two seconds to hear the delayed roar from the people standing back by the tee.

When Phil birdied #12, the response from the gallery sounded like an eagle roar, not a birdie roar.

Gary McBride, Amy's Dad

Now I'm pumping my fist as I walk off the green. I've answered Ernie, I'm only two down, and I've got #13, another birdie hole, coming up.

Now I know I can make this thing happen. "This is my day!" I keep saying to myself. "This is my day!"

129

PLAYER	SCORE	HOLE
Els	−7	13
Mickelson	−5	12
Langer	−4	12
Choi	−4	13
Garcia	−3	18
Couples	−3	16
DiMarco	−3	11

Azalea
Par 5
510 Yards
Dogleg Left

The 13th (a par 5 with a big dogleg left that I can reach in two) is by far my favorite hole at Augusta because the shot dispersion sets up much better for a lefty than for a right-handed golfer. It's just so much easier to hit a big fade around the dogleg corner than it is to try and hook it. So #13 sets up perfectly for me. This is also one of the most scenic holes on the course.

Heading up to the tee box, I get to walk across the Byron Nelson Bridge. Another great legend, Mr. Nelson once won eleven tournaments in a row. It's a record equivalent to Joe DiMaggio's 56-game hitting streak in baseball. I don't think either will ever be broken. Back in 1996, I won the Byron Nelson Classic and had a chance to spend some time with Mr. Nelson. At his house, he has a woodworking shop where he spends a lot of his time. I noticed that he has great sensitivity and touch with his hands. It's easy to see why he was known for having a great touch with his iron shots around the green. I've always enjoyed being around Mr. Nelson because of the gentleman he is and the way he treats people so kindly.

Up on the tee, I line my feet up far to the right. I want the ball to go over the tree limbs and across the creek up in the fairway. I make a good swing and the ball starts way right, then cuts around the corner. It lands in the perfect spot. I'll have less than 200 yards and a 7-iron in.

As soon as I hit my tee shot, I hear a big roar off in the distance. But this one is so far away, I know it's not from one of the leaders— so it couldn't really matter. It turns out the roar was for Padraig Harrington who hit a hole-in-one on #16. It's the first ace in the Masters since Raymond Floyd did it back in 1996. There's that Masters magic rising up!

As we were crossing over the fairway, one of the course marshals who works in the same spot every year came up and started hugging Phil's parents and me. "Relax, it's okay," he said. "Ernie's in the trees on #14. He's going to make bogey at best."

Amy Mickelson

As I'm walking down the fairway, I can't help but admire the beauty surrounding me. There are a couple thousand azaleas all around this hole—lining the fairways, surrounding the green. It's just beautiful.

Someone from the crowd yells out that Ernie Els is in the rough at #14. And I think, "Even in the midst of all this beauty, you can still find yourself in a tough spot."

I'm also very glad to be heading away from Amen Corner. Some people say it can be a picturesque grave for many championship dreams.

Others say you should whisper a silent prayer when you finally get it behind you.

Amen.

Something else happened in 2003 that Amy and I rarely talk about. In fact, we didn't mention it to anybody other than family and very close friends for nearly a year. I'm so very fortunate to have the life I have. I'm able to provide very well for my family while doing what I love to do. But similar to Amen Corner at Augusta, even in the midst of all the beauty in my life, I found myself in a very rough spot on March 23, 2003. That was the day our son, Evan, was born.

Amy's pregnancy started off normal enough. She was due to give birth during the first week of March—which coincided with the Ford Championship tournament. I had just signed with Ford as a new sponsor and was looking forward to participating. But I decided to stay with Amy so I wouldn't miss Evan's birth.

The baby, however, didn't arrive that week. And during the tournament, Steve Lyons (the president of Ford), was asked at a press conference why I wasn't there. His response was simple and to the point: "Phil's wife, Amy, is about to give birth and he's with her," said Steve. "That's why he represents our company—he puts family first. Phil is where he should be and he's where we want him to be." After I heard that kind of support, I knew I had a special relationship with the perfect company for me.

After waiting another two weeks, the doctors finally decided to bring Amy to the hospital to induce labor. She was given an epidural and when they went in to break her water, they found a large amount of scar tissue that had formed from Sophia's birth. Our doctor told us that the scar tissue was the reason the baby was late—because he couldn't break through. As Amy started to deliver, it was fairly calm in the maternity ward at that moment. So one of the nurses went downstairs to the Emergency Room and brought back a special kit that is used just in case a new baby has trouble breathing. I don't know why she did it—if it was routine or if she just had a feeling it might be needed. But the fact is she probably saved Evan's life.

———————

We thought it was going to be routine. They had given Amy an epidural, so I kissed her and went in the other room. "I'll see you in an hour," I said, "and we'll get to see this new baby."

Renee McBride, Amy's Mom

———————

No sooner had the doctor cut through the scar tissue and broken Amy's water when, all of a sudden, the baby was born. Evan came so fast and so abruptly, however, that it apparently shocked his system—and the doctor couldn't get him to breathe or cry. In essence, my son was stillborn.

The nurses took him over to a table, pulled out the emergency kit, and started putting tubes down his throat. "We're pumping oxygen into his body so that air will get to his brain," one of them said. They were trying to get him to wake up and breathe. But nothing was happening.

I leaned over him and started whispering in his ear, "Breathe, Evan, breathe. Breathe, Evan, breathe." But there was no response.

After a little while, I started yelling, "Come on, Evan. Breathe.

Breathe, Evan, breathe." A full seven minutes went by. It seemed like an eternity. They were just getting ready to hook him up to a respirator when finally, at last, he took his first breath and started to cry. I was so thankful and so relieved. But then the nurse said: "He's not out of the woods, yet. It'll take awhile before we know. We've got to keep him breathing and crying."

I went over to Amy to let her know that he was breathing. But there was a huge pool of blood just below her—and she appeared paler than I'd ever seen a person look. Having been at the births of our two other children, I knew this was not normal. "She's bleeding profusely," said the doctor. "With all that scar tissue, the baby must have caused a tear in her uterus. It's really bad. It might be the main artery." Then the doctor turned to the other nurses. "Let's take her down to OR," she said. "Now! Now!"

From where we were in the waiting room, we could hear Phil yelling, "Breathe, Evan, breathe!" Then the doctors and nurses started running back and forth and all over the place. It was hysteria.

Phil finally came out and said that Evan was breathing now, but they had to take Amy down to the operating room at the other end of the hall. When they first came out, all the nurses were screaming: "Get out of the hall! Get out of the way!" They wheeled Amy right past us and I could see that she was incoherent and her face was gray. I started to cry.

Renee McBride

One of the nurses told me that they had to page a specialist for this type of surgery. "You can't just go in there and sew up a tear," she said. "Only a few surgeons are trained to do this. It's a very intricate procedure where they actually have to insert something into the artery. Normally we'd perform an immediate hysterectomy—but we can't because she's already lost way too much blood."

I left the family waiting room and went back into the hallway. I tried to go into the operating room to be with Amy, but they wouldn't let me in. So I stood outside and looked through a little window and could hear the nurses talking about her being in what they called "hemorrhaging shock."

Then I thought about Evan. I had left him back down at the other end of the hall—and I didn't know if he was going to be okay. So I walked down there and stuck my head in the door. The doctor and nurses were still working on him. There were tubes all over the place. "He's fighting hard for his life," one of them said. So I just stepped back out in the hall and sat down on a bench.

I remember looking down this long, sterile hallway and seeing Phil sitting on a bench all by himself. His head was in his hands and he was looking down.

He got up and went down to Amy's side of the hall. Then back down to Evan. Then back to Amy again. Finally, he sat down on the bench outside Amy's door.

He didn't know what to do or which way to go. I wanted to help him so much, but there was nothing I could do or say.

So I stood outside the door where they were working on Evan and kept watch on my nephew.

Tina Mickelson, Phil's Sister

Philip normally has a quiet confidence about him. But not at that moment. He was just lost. And we were all scared to death.

Mary Mickelson, Phil's Mom

The specialist they were looking for had been driving to dinner and was only three minutes away from the hospital when he received the page. He ran by me and went right into Amy's room. I got up and paced back and forth for a while. At one point, I stopped right next to an intersecting hallway. Two of the nurses were around the corner whispering to each other. They didn't know I was there. "It's just so sad, isn't it," one of them said, "that those three little children are going to grow up without their mother."

I went over and sat down outside Amy's room and just prayed and prayed that she'd be all right, and that Evan would be all right. I said I would do certain things, if only they would live. I made promises. At that moment, I would have done anything in the world to switch places with Amy.

The next hour was the longest, most agonizing hour of my life. It seemed like it would never end. And as much as I'd like to, it's an hour I will never forget.

Finally, at long last, the doctor came out of the operating room and said: "She's stable now. I think we saved her." I couldn't believe it. I've never had such a feeling of relief and gratitude. Then I went down to Evan (because I still wasn't allowed to see Amy)—and the doctors and nurses in his room said they were now optimistic about his chances.

They put Amy in the adult Intensive Care Unit and Evan in the neo-natal ICU. The next morning, the doctors told me that our son did not appear to have any brain damage due to a lack of oxygen nor were there any signs of adverse side effects. He was going to be okay. Amy stayed in the ICU for three or four days—but got stronger with each day that passed.

The next morning when I came in to see Amy, a nurse said to me: "I was so happy when I saw your daughter's name on the charts this morning. When I went home last night, all I could think of were those poor little children without a mother. She was literally bleeding to death, and when that kind of complication happens in childbirth, it's almost always fatal. That doctor did a miraculous job."

Renee McBride

They moved Amy up to a room on the maternity ward and brought Evan in to us. I can't tell you how wonderful it was to see my wife holding my son—both healthy, both in good spirits. I never felt so good. It's my mental picture of happiness. Joy is the word for Evan.

Phil stayed in the hospital the entire time—even when Evan and I were in intensive care. When they moved me to the maternity ward, he slept on this tiny little cot and his legs were sticking off it by at least a foot. I knew he was uncomfortable, but he refused to leave me alone.

Amy Mickelson

I was visiting Phil and Amy in the hospital just before she and Evan were released. Amy had to go down for some final tests, so Phil and I were left in the room together.

We turned on the television and some sports commentators were talking about Phil not being at that week's tournament. They said that he seemed to have lost his passion for the game and they made some lousy comments about him not having his priorities straight.

I remember being very angry about that. But it didn't seem to bother Phil. I think he felt that if they had known the real situation, they never would have made those remarks.

Tina Mickelson

We finally got Amy and Evan home from the hospital but, of course, the trauma of the entire event lingered on. While Amy was recuperating, I just hung around the house not knowing what to do with myself. So she told me to go play in the Atlanta Classic and get ready for the Masters. I went, but my heart just wasn't in it—and I missed the cut. The next week was the Masters and Amy wanted me to go there, too. But I was playing so poorly that I didn't touch a club for five days before teeing off at Augusta because I was so tired of hitting bad shots. Amazingly, I still managed to finish a quiet third place in the tournament. Over the course of those two tournaments, I never said a word to anybody, especially the media, about what had happened. It was just too hard to talk about.

At the end of November, Amy was fully recovered and we took the opportunity to have a heart-to-heart talk. "We had a very tough year," she said, "and we can't keep reliving it. Amanda, Sophia, and Evan are healthy and doing great. Let's just stay home for the last month of the year and be together. Then, in January, you can get with Rick Smith and Dave Pelz and start work. Put your trust in them. They're good friends and they know what they're doing. And when 2004 rolls around, no more looking back. 2003 will be history." Amy and I are a partnership. We discuss everything. That particular conversation, and her advice to put things behind us and start moving forward, really, really helped me.

January came around and I excitedly dove into my game with Rick and Dave. And wouldn't you know it, I won the very first tournament of the year, the Bob Hope Desert Classic. On Sunday, I managed to make a birdie at the 18th hole to tie Skip Kendall at 30 under par. Then I made a birdie on the first playoff hole to win it.

During one of the media interviews, I mentioned publicly for the first time what had happened during Evan's birth (without going into a lot of detail). It just kind of slipped out. I didn't say much because I don't like to talk about it—and I sincerely ask that people don't bring it up to me again.

It was the second time in three years that I had won the Hope Classic. At the time, I thought about the irony of the title.

Hope.

In the fairway at #13, I think I have landed it in the perfect spot. But when I get out there, I see that I have to contend with an uneven lie. This should be no problem, but I also have to think about the area around the green, which is particularly treacherous. There is water close to the right edge where the tributary winds down. When I played this hole on Friday, I pulled my approach shot and it rolled off the green but stopped inches above Rae's Creek. With some luck, I still managed a birdie, though.

In the back of my mind, I remember what happened to Curtis Strange back in 1985. He was leading the tournament when he knocked his approach shot from the thirteenth fairway into the water. Then he did it again on #15 and knocked himself out of the tournament.

I've seen Phil play many rounds of golf. I could tell he was really grinding out there. He was working very hard. But he didn't show it to the people on the course. He just kept smiling.

Gary McBride, Amy's Dad

"Okay," I'm thinking, "I went nuts on #12 and went straight at the flag. But this is not the time to go right at it. It's a time to give myself a 20-footer for eagle to tie for the lead—or a short putt for birdie and be only one back with five holes to go." So I pull out my seven-iron and try to hit the left side of the green. I'm going to take the right side (and thereby the water hazard) out of play. I make a good swing and my ball lands in the middle of the green, catches the swale, and rolls down to within 20 feet.

I remember turning to Amy and saying: "He's under such control. How much more can a person prepare? This is all part of the habit that's been created all year. This is what he's worked so hard for."

Rick Smith, Phil's Long-Game Coach

There's a leaderboard right behind the green on #13—so I understand exactly where I stand and what this putt means. If I make it for eagle, I tie for the lead. If I two-putt for a birdie, I'll be only one back.

Walking around the green, I know this putt breaks eight inches more than it looks. For whatever reason, the ball snaps hard to the right when it reaches the hole. I've missed this putt low many times in the past, so I'm going to make sure that, this time, I play enough break. As I set up to make my stroke, I'm playing it to break even more than my eyes tell me it will break. I'm aiming a good three feet outside the left edge. I'm also going to make certain I don't hit it too hard. I want it to catch the break.

My putting stroke feels good and I send the ball way out there. It starts swinging, swinging, swinging back and . . . . . I miss it low and it rolls two or three feet by the hole. I didn't hit it hard enough.

That darn putt! Every year I play more and more break, and I miss it by less and less. One of these days, I'm going to make it!

Now I'm within my three-foot circle. I've hit so many thousands of these all year, it's not even a second thought. I don't take it for granted, though. I step up and knock it in for birdie.

Ernie saved par on #14. The way I look at it, though, we both stood on the 13th tee at five under par. He eagled the hole, I birdied it. Chris DiMarco also made birdie. He's now only three off the pace.

Okay. Five holes to go. I'm one shot down.

PLAYER	SCORE	HOLE
Els	−7	14
Mickelson	−6	13
Choi	−5	14
Langer	−4	13
DiMarco	−4	13
Garcia	−3	18
Couples	−3	17
Casey	−2	13
Singh	−2	18
Love III	−2	17
Price	−1	17
Triplett	E	15
Wittenberg (A)	E	18
Howell III	E	18
Goosen	E	18

Chinese Fir
Par 4
440 Yards
Slight Dogleg Left

*T*his is the only hole at Augusta without bunkers—and it sets up very well for me. The fairway is higher than the tee box and I want to carry it over the ridge 290 yards out, so I decide to hit a big, high-cut driver.

I aim down the right side again. And I absolutely rip at it as hard as I can. The ball ends up over the ridge, right in the middle of the fairway. Perfect shot.

But then, as we're walking off the tee, I hear another huge roar. I can't tell if it was at #15 or #16 green. I don't think it's Ernie, but I'm certainly not sure. What's going on?

We heard the roar and it sounded like an eagle. It was almost hysterical in nature. What was it? Did Ernie make another birdie? What? Then somebody told us that Kirk Triplett had just made a hole-in-one at #16. Two holes-in-one on the back nine at Augusta on Sunday! Wow! The Masters Magic! It's really happening! What's next?

Amy Mickelson

———

In the fairway, I'm mulling over my 148-yard approach shot. The green terraces down sharply from left to right, so I must carry over the first tier. Fortunately, the pin placement is the easiest it could possibly be—in a low spot where all the balls collect. Another birdie possibility.

Bones and I are talking over the shot when we hear another huge roar—and this time there was no doubt. Ernie Els had birdied the 15th hole. Now he's two shots ahead.

This shot is now more critical than ever. I was thinking about hitting a 9-iron, flying it in low about 142 yards, and having it land four yards short of the hole. But Bones has a different idea. "We should hit a pitching wedge," he says. "Hit it a little fuller and a little higher. We still have to take six or seven yards off of it, but we can bring it in a little softer. And I think we'll have a better chance of getting close."

That is such an astute recommendation that I can't do anything but agree. Bones' imagination and knowledge of my game really pays off at this moment.

It was an advantage seeing what Ernie had done in front of me. After his last birdie, it was clear to me that he was not going to give me anything. Now I know that I really have to dig deep. I'm pumped up and I'm going to fire right at that pin.

As I stand behind the ball, I look toward the green and visualize where the ball is going to land. I take a couple of long, lazy, fluid practice swings. Standing over this shot, I know that I have to take 7 yards off this pitching wedge. All the hours of work I spent with Dave Pelz, the thousands and thousands of shots I hit getting the yardages down with the wedges—now it was going to pay off.

I hit it. It feels good. "Be right," I say. "C'mon." The shot bounces on the front of the green, and slowly rolls right toward the flagstick.

My ball misses going in the cup by an inch and stops a half-foot past the hole. What a great feeling! I've got a tap-in for birdie!

———————

When Phil almost holed that shot, I was thinking "This is his day! This is his day!" I just knew it! And I started to cry. My girlfriend Tricia looked at me and said: "You better not start that right now—because we're all going to lose it if you do. You have four holes to go. Pull yourself together."

Amy Mickelson

———————

Now there's another huge roar at Augusta—only this time it's coming from our hole, the 14th. But it sounds more like a roar for eagle than one for birdie. And I know Ernie heard it.

When I make those long, lazy, fluid practice swings before I hit a shot, I'm not limbering up my muscles as many people believe. Rather, I'm visualizing what the swing feels like for the shot I'm trying to create. The neuromuscular message that is sent from your brain to your body during a golf swing is what I'm trying to focus on. I don't believe in muscle memory because I don't believe your muscles have memory. I believe that our mind can be trained to tell our muscles what to do. And so, if I visualize a good golf swing—and create that feeling in my body—I will ultimately have a better chance of hitting my desired shot. In other words, the neuromuscular message that is sent from your brain during an imaginary swing is as important as the actual swing itself. So, visualization first, then the real swing.

A proper visualization routine works not only in golf, but in other areas of my life. That tango I was able to pull off with Amy at our wedding was a good example. At six foot, three inches tall—and with size 13 feet—I'm obviously not the greatest dancer in the world. But I actually spent more time visualizing that dance routine than I did practicing it. And as Amy will tell you, I pulled it off.

This entire concept involving visualization affects my regular golf routine—how I practice, how often I practice, when I practice, and when I don't practice. After playing a competitive round of golf, for instance, many of the pros will go straight to the driving range—especially if they did not have a good round. But that doesn't work for me. After spending five hours on the golf course and then doing an hour and a half of media interviews, I'm tired. So after the round, I'll go somewhere by myself and think about the day's round. I'll try to figure out what it is that I need to do differently—or what I need to work on to improve for the next day. I'll imagine hitting good shots instead of bad ones. If I have a problem and can't figure out why, I'll pick up the phone and call Rick Smith or Dave Pelz. "Why am I hooking the ball?" I'll ask. "Why am I missing it left?" "What's wrong with my putting stroke?"

I'll also think about all those factors I went over the week before the tournament—density, altitude, temperature, relative humidity, whether I was playing in the morning or the afternoon, things like that. In the mornings, when the temperatures are cooler, players often come up short of the green on their approach shots. But in the afternoons, if the temperature hits, say, 90 degrees, the ball will fly farther. Taking into account extraneous factors such as temperature can make the difference in winning or losing a golf tournament.

Walking away from the golf course after I play a round just works for me. But it obviously doesn't work that way for everybody. Ben Hogan felt he had to hit 500 golf balls a day in order to keep his edge. I felt that way when I was a kid. But after I became a professional, I started to experiment and try different things.

Right after I came out on the Tour, I had a conversation with Jack Nicklaus about preparing for the major golf tournaments. He told me that he always took off the week before a major. I tried that a number of times, but ended up performing terribly. I felt stale, a little nervous—and I always started slow. Jack's routine just didn't work for me. So now, I always play the week before a major. It keeps my game sharp, my competitive edge tuned up—and that, I believe, increases my chances of success.

Interestingly enough, while a short layoff before major tournaments doesn't work well for me, a long layoff in the off-season does. I've had some of my best outings after not having touched a golf club for six weeks. A good example was the 2004 Grand Slam of Golf in Hawaii. I hadn't touched a club in more than three weeks when I went in there and shot a 59 on the final day and won the tournament. And I didn't touch another club until January 1, 2005—five weeks later.

I like the long layoff in the off-season. It gives me a chance to spend more time with Amy and the children. And that, in turn, puts me in a better emotional frame of mind when I do end up going back out on the Tour.

After Phil has laid off golf for more than a month in the off-season, he'll start to get this itch to compete, to get back in the arena. It's an interesting thing to watch. He's like a little kid who's standing on the sidelines while all his teammates are playing in the game and he's not. He just can't wait to get back in there and compete.

Amy Mickelson

Sometimes the media will criticize me for taking so much time off. For instance, I normally do not play in the Mercedes Championship during the first week of January. And people will say that I'm not being supportive of the Tour. Well, the Mercedes tournament is a great event because the field includes all the previous year's winners who compete for $5 million in prize money. But for me, money isn't everything. Besides, during the first week of January, my kids are still on break and it's a chance for me to extend the holidays and be with them. Not only that, but the longer layoff has become part of a routine that works best for me.

Young golfers often ask me about my golf routine. And of course, I'll explain it to them in some detail. But I'll always end by reminding them that what worked for Ben Hogan or Jack Nicklaus might not work for them. Hogan and Nicklaus were great golfers because they had their own ways of doing things. So I'll advise young people to find out what works best for them. That, I think, is the best way to achieve your own success.

Of course, when I get back to golf after the off-season, I *really* get back. I'll go down to the Callaway Test Center and isolate myself over at one end. I'm not there to chat or pal around with anyone— I'm there to practice. Rick Smith and Dave Pelz will also fly into town to work with me on virtually all the elements of my game. I'll go from a no-hour workday to a 12- or 14-hour workday. I'll hit 1,500 golf balls a day—wedges, short-irons, long-irons, drivers, three-woods. I'll do my chipping around the green with certain little practice targets that I'll have to hit. I'll spend time in the bunkers. And I'll do my hundred putts from a three-foot circle.

I was once asked why I putt in a circle around the hole. Well, as the 1957 Masters champion, Jackie Burke, once told me, golf is a game of circles. The hole is a circle, the ball is a circle, the greens are circles, and many of the bunkers are circles. When you go out to a course and play, they even call it a "round" of golf. And since your target is a circle, you should practice in a circle. So that's why I put in a circle around the hole.

In some way, I believe my strategy of stepping away from golf for an extended period of time relates back to our family vacations when my dad used to stop at the peak of the fun. I always wanted to get back to the ski slopes, for instance, because I always had such a great time skiing.

Of course, that's what golf is for me—great fun. I was fortunate enough to be reminded of that in early 2004 by Dave Pelz.

―――――――――――

About a month before the Masters, we were having a casual conversation when I mentioned to Phil that I thought he looked too serious on Sundays. "When you are at the top of your game, you're smiling and laughing," I said. "When you play with your friends, you are almost unbeatable—because you are enjoying yourself. That allows your mind and body to perform at the top of your game. If you try to be too serious, it's like tying one hand behind your back. Phil, you need to lighten up on Sundays."

At first, Phil looked at me like I was crazy. But then he thought about it. And I think he realized that all of his best final rounds occurred when he was having fun—not when he was being too serious.

Dave Pelz, Phil's Short-Game Coach

As I walk up to the 14th green, I know I have a tap in for a birdie—and I'm feeling good. The fans are excited and applauding. I smile and nod. "Thank you," I say, even though I know they can't hear me.

That smile and nod that Phil flashes is, I think, the mark of a really fine human being. It's almost as if he's embarrassed by all the applause and he's trying to be polite in how he responds to it.

Phil Mickelson, Sr., Phil's Dad

I was taking care of the kids at our rental house not far from the course. When Phil birdied #14, I figured it was time to get the kids over there because their daddy just might win this thing. "Amanda," I said, "are you ready to go to Daddy's work now?"

"No, I don't think I want to go today," she replied. Amanda was having too much Easter fun.

"Well, I think it's going to be a special day," I said, trying to convince her to go. "I think you'll want to be there. And he'll want you there."

"No, I don't want to. I want to stay here."

Renee McBride, Amy's Mom

It's a gimme putt. I tap it in and head over to #15. Now I've really got some momentum going. Three birdies in a row. Still down by one.

PLAYER	SCORE	HOLE
Els	−8	15
Mickelson	−7	14
Choi	−5	14
Langer	−5	14
DiMarco	−4	14
Garcia	−3	18
Couples	−2	18

Firethorn
Par 5
500 Yards

T he 15th hole at Augusta is a straightaway par 5 that is reachable in two. Golfing historians remember it as the sight of Gene
Sarazen's 1935 "Shot Heard Round the World"—when he holed
his second shot from the fairway for a miraculous double eagle.

#15, however, presents a very tough tee shot for me. There are trees
just off the tee box that prevent me from going with the fade shot that I've
been hitting most of the day. Now I've got to try to hook a driver—something I haven't done since the eleventh hole. I know that if I miss it right
into the trees, I'll have no second shot. So if I miss, it must be to the left
where at least I'll have a recovery shot and still a chance for birdie.

On the tee, I line up my feet to the left, square my shoulders, and try
to hit the inside part of the ball so it will draw. My swing feels fairly
good, but I hold on to it and the ball doesn't really draw at all. It hangs
out way to the left and rolls into the first cut of trees.

As I'm walking up the fairway, I know that I probably don't have a
shot to the green. And I recall how, a couple of years ago, I went for the
green in two, but the ball caught the fringe and rolled back into the water.

I made a double bogey and finished third, and didn't enjoy the Q&A following the round.

When I get up to my ball, I see that maybe it's better than I originally thought. As I look toward the green, I see two tall pine trees about ten yards up on my right, a smaller one in the center about twenty yards up, and three big pines on the left. And of course, there's a good-sized pond in front of the green. If I go for it, the trees prevent me from getting the ball to climb up over the water to the green. Hmmm, I might be able to go low, though.

In the past, I've had very similar shots with vastly different outcomes.

———

In 1992, when Phil was still in college and again leading while trying to defend his championship at the Tucson Open, he drove his ball into the trees left of the third hole. I immediately reached for an 8-iron and tried to hand it to him. "No, Coach," he said, "give me a 3-iron."

"Phil!" I said. "We're 148 yards from the green and there's no way you can hit it through the trees and over the water. You just don't have a shot. We're only 25 yards from the fairway. We're leading by two shots! C'mon! Just chip it back into the fairway. We can make par."

Meanwhile, I was covering the bag with my arms so he couldn't reach in there and get another club. But Phil kind of moved me out of the way and grabbed the 3-iron anyway.

"Get away," he said. Then Phil quickly addressed the ball and *Whack!* he hit it. And as God is my witness, his ball went through the trees, skipped twice across the water, and rolled up onto the back of the green.

Phil, however, wasn't as thrilled as I was.

"What's wrong?" I asked. "We're on the green. It was a great shot."

"Coach," he said, "if it had skipped three times, we'd be right next to the pin!"

Coach Steve Loy, Phil's Business Manager

⸻

In Sunday's final round at the 2002 Bay Hill Invitational (which is Arnold Palmer's tournament), Philip was trailing Tiger Woods by one shot when he came to the par 5 16th hole. (Tiger was playing in the group behind him.)

Philip hit his tee shot into the trees on the far right side of the fairway. Knowing that Tiger would probably birdie the hole, he decided to try to reach the green by going through the trees and over the water. Actually, he had a pretty clear path through the trees and I've seen him pull off shots like this one before. But he didn't hit the ball hard enough and it plunked into the water. He made bogey and Tiger won the tournament.

The media really hammered him for taking such a risk. But after the tournament, Arnold Palmer came out and defended Philip. "The boy had one shot—and he made the right decision," said Arnie. "You guys need to back off!"

Arnie also sent a note to Philip afterward. "You never would have won as many tournaments as you have by playing a more conservative game," he wrote. "Keep playing to win. Keep charging. Your majors will come."

Phil Mickelson, Sr., Phil's Dad

157

When we saw Phil behind the ball and looking toward the green, we all started saying: "Use your veto, Bones. Don't let him go for it. Make him lay it up. Use your veto."

Amy Mickelson, Phil's Wife

As I'm looking through the trees toward the green, I realize that I really do have to lay up—which is okay. I'd spent so much time working with Dave Pelz from inside 150 yards, so much time controlling the distance the ball flies and how much spin it has after it lands, that I am confident I'll still have a good chance to make birdie.

Bones and I also talk about the fact that the pin placement on this hole is very favorable. All I really have to do is punch the ball down in front of the water. Then I'm going to have a 70 percent chance of birdie and, at worst, a par.

So I take an 8-iron and just chip it 120 yards right down the fairway. Now I have only a 75-yard wedge shot to the green.

There are shots where you can win a tournament—and there are shots where you can *not* win a tournament. This was a shot where Phil could *not* win the tournament. But if he had tried to blow the ball over the green to get in that back right bunker, he could have *lost* the Masters. If you can lose, but you can't win—why try it?

Dave Pelz, Phil's Short-Game Coach

This was a very difficult shot at a very crucial time. "Old Phil" might have "gone for it" and pulled it off. But "New Phil" laid up. And that was the right call. He had just birdied #12, #13, and #14. No sense pushing his luck.

As Phil has become a more experienced player, he knows what he is capable of—more so than when he was always taking those riskier shots. Phil was now combining "Old Phil" and "New Phil." He was demonstrating the balance that all the great players have—to know when the risks are rewarding and when the risks are defeating. It was very rewarding for me, personally, to see Phil demonstrating a nice mix between conservative and aggressive play.

Coach Steve Loy

For my approach shot to the green, I take some spin off the ball because I think it will land soft. It lands in the perfect spot, but hits harder than I expect—and rolls twelve feet beyond the flagstick.

Most of the greens were hitting pretty soft, but this one landed a little bit firmer. I really don't know why because this green is in the low part of Augusta, which typically makes the greens softer from all the water draining down. The higher greens—like #9 and #18—tend to be firmer. Anyway, I played the ball to land soft and it ended up taking a harder bounce. But it's okay, because I still have a good look at birdie to tie for the lead. At worst, I'll make par.

Up on the green, I have a quick putt with a decent amount of break—left to right. Unfortunately, I don't hit the greatest putt. I miss *low to the right and it runs a couple of feet by. But it's in my circle and I'm not worried about it. I tap in for par.*

Three birdies in a row and now par. At this point, all of us were living and dying on every shot—and we were hoping that the magic would continue.

Amy Mickelson

"Abracadabra. Alakazam. My girls have been good. Please make lots of tickets appear under the table." That's what I say when Amanda, Sophia, and I are sitting down at Chuck E. Cheese's after we've just come out of the arcade area. I have the girls close their eyes and, while I'm saying the magic words and rubbing the table, all the tickets we've won will suddenly move from my back pocket and materialize under the table. Then Sophia and Amanda will open their eyes, look under the table, and find all the tickets.

"Daddy, use your magic, again," they say. "Use your magic, again."

"You can only use your magic so often," I'll tell them. "Later, if you're good, I can give you some of my magic—and you can use it, too." Then my daughters will take all their magically produced tickets up to the counter and redeem them for prizes.

Whenever I'm at home for a week or more, I'll take my girls on Daddy/Daughter Dates. Chuck E. Cheese is one of our favorite places to go. Usually, it'll be just me and either Amanda or Sophia. Sometimes both of them will go with me (we call those Daddy/

Daughter-Daughter Dates). The idea is to give each of them some individual time—and to have fun while we're out. Sometimes we go to the park, sometimes to Lego Land, or wherever the kids suggest. Of course, I don't forget Amy. She and I go out on a date at least once a week—usually to dinner and a movie. But we'll also do some outdoor activities just to be together and have fun. Also, now that my son, Evan, is growing up a little bit, he's catching on to the routine I have with his sisters. He'll run to the door as we're about to leave and, in his own little way, ask to go along. So I started taking him on his own father-son dates.

Now you might think that, as a pro golfer, I'm always taking my kids to the golf course. But actually, it's only recently that I've done anything with the kids that involves golf. And that started when Sophia had just turned two years old. "Daddy," she said, "I want to go golf with you." So I took her to the driving range on one of our dates.

Since then, Amanda has asked the same thing. We'll go out to the driving range and hit maybe 15 or 20 balls. Then we drive the cart and I let one of the girls sit on my lap and steer. Next, we might go out on the course to a lake. I'll bring about ten old golf balls and let them hit the balls into the lake so they can watch the splashes. I try to keep those outings short so the kids won't get bored and instead, will enjoy them each time. There's another lesson from my parents making it full circle. Stop the activity at the peak of the fun.

I once asked Amanda what she thought I liked to do best. I thought she was going to say golf, but she didn't. She said the thing I like best in the world was to take her and Sophia out on Daddy/Daughter Dates. And the next best thing, she said, was to give them my magic.

I can make my daddy disappear in one second. He stands behind the curtain and I say, "Abracadabra, alakazam." Then I
count up to 40 with my eyes closed. And when I open the
curtain, he's gone. Then he reappears on the floor behind the
couch with his head on a pillow. He's asleep, he's snoring, and
he doesn't remember how he got there.

Amanda Mickelson, Phil's daughter

In addition to granting my children the power of magic, I will
also take it away when they misbehave. "Every parent has control
over their children's magic," I'll say to the kids. "You have to act
good and be responsible because magic is very powerful. If you're
not good and not responsible, I'll have to take it away for a couple
of days."

And I do take it away if they're misbehaving. Amanda, as the
oldest, has been through it many times before. If she has a little
tantrum or doesn't want to go to bed when it's time, I'll take her
magic away. That could be in the form of her silkies or her stuffed
animals. Or she won't be able to make daddy disappear from behind the curtains. And I'll always make it her choice.

"I don't want to take your magic away," I'll say. "But if you
choose to not be good, then the magic just won't be there."

*Walking to the sixteenth tee, I'm keeping a close eye on Ernie Els to
see what he is doing. He isn't backing up at all. But at least he's not*

pulling away, either. I'm also thinking that the last three holes at Augusta are not historically birdie holes. But today, there are very susceptible pin placements on all of them. I feel I can birdie at least one to tie. And if I can birdie two, I might be able to win the tournament. I just keep believing that something good is going to happen.

One shot down. Three to go.

PLAYER	SCORE	HOLE
Els	–8	16
Mickelson	–7	15
Choi	–6	16
DiMarco	–4	13
Langer	–3	15

Redbud
Par 3
170 Yards

*O*kay, here we are at the hole where, this afternoon, there have been two holes-in-one within ten minutes of each other. First Padraig Harrington did it, then Kirk Triplett.

The pin is down on the left side of the green where all the balls funnel. I know I can make birdie today—but by no means will it be an easy birdie. Three bunkers surround the green and there is water all down the left side. It's also a hard shot for me because the green sets up for a right-handed shot dispersion—just the opposite of #12. If I leave it short left, I'll be in the water—and long right would leave me up on the hill with an unlikely two-putt.

This is also not the greatest hole for me, historically. In 2001, I hooked a seven iron above the hole that resulted in a three-putt bogey and killed my chances of winning. And earlier this week, I hit the ball way to the right and ended up making double bogey. Going into today's final round, I had made only two bogeys and that one double bogey here on #16.

I'm thinking about all of this when I walk up to the tee box. Bones and I have a casual conversation about the wind. He notices that it's blowing *in our faces—and we both know when that happens on #16, it doesn't seem to affect the flight of the ball as much as it does on other holes. So we're not going to let that fool us. We are going to hit the club we would hit even if there was no wind.*

For me to get at this pin, I have to take a very aggressive swing. If I miss it left, it'll go short and I'll be in the water. And I sure don't want to miss it right and have to contend with coming down that slope.

On this tee shot, I'm not shooting for the best miss. I'm going for it. I know there's no alternative. I've just got to do it. Ernie's not backing up. I'm a shot down—and I am going to attack this flagstick.

We love "New Phil." But it's always nice to know that "Old Phil" is in reserve as our secret weapon when needed.

Amy Mickelson

Too many players fear failure. But as much as Phil dislikes defeat and disappointment, he does not fear failure. He's a freewheeling, "go for it" player. That's why he's won so many championships in his life. I never want to see that change.

Coach Steve Loy

Initially, I think I'll hit a 7-iron and not take a full swing. But Bones disagrees: "No, this is not the time for that," he says. "We need to hit the

8. We want it coming in softer. We want it drawing rather than fading. It's time for a full 8-iron."

"All right, Bones," I say. "Let's go with an 8."

I take a full swing and start the ball left of the pin. It draws right, just like I want it to do. It hits just short of the pin, catches the ridge, rolls down underneath the hole, and stops 18 feet away. I'll have a very make-able putt from down there. As a matter of fact, it's an easy putt. It only breaks about six or eight inches and is uphill.

I turn to Bones and say, "Good club."

I had been thinking about that tee shot all year. I wanted Phil to stand on the #16 tee box and feel that he could hit it close to the hole without having any fear at all. A right-handed golfer would typically love to hit a draw into the flagstick because he doesn't have to contend with the lake on the left. But a left-handed golfer, if he's going to hook it, will have to sweep it over the lake and draw it back. That, to say the least, is a risky shot.

But Phil hit a beautiful little hook. That one swing, I think, said more about his development over the past year than any other shot he hit at the Masters.

Rick Smith, Phil's Long-Game Coach

Walking down to the 16th green was an awesome feeling. I'd lost a little momentum on the previous hole, but I could just sense that something good was going to happen. People were standing, applauding, and holding their fists in the air. "C'mon, Phil!" "Let's see some magic!"

And that's exactly what I'm thinking. The magic was taken away on #15. Now I want it back.

I believe my mom and dad must get a real kick out of seeing me deal with my daughter Sophia. My parents tell me I was a strong-willed child. I didn't want to put my napkin in my lap at the dinner table. When they said go right, I would go left. When I was out of their sight, I did my own thing—like run away from home. Well, you know that circle of life—what goes around comes around. With Sophia and me, it's one strong-willed kid against another. The word patience is meant for Sophia. Let me give you a couple of examples that occurred all within a week of each other.

When Sophia was two years old, we were just packing up to go home from a tournament. Rather than staying in a hotel, this time Amy and I had rented a house in a nice little residential neighborhood not far from the golf course. As we were cleaning the house to leave it in as good a condition as when we'd moved in, I started hearing sirens in the distance. They got closer and closer—and the next thing I knew there were police cars, fire trucks, and an ambulance pulling into our driveway. All the policemen, the firemen, and the paramedics rushed up to the house. "What's wrong? What's wrong?" I kept asking them.

Well, it turned out Sophia had wandered into the kitchen, gotten up on a chair, and started playing with the security alarm. And she didn't push just one button. She pushed them all—police, fire, emergency. Of course, I apologized profusely and signed autographs for all the firefighters, policemen, and paramedics. And while I was doing that, Sophia grabbed a black Sharpie pen and scribbled all over the ottoman in the living room.

After that, we began watching her much more carefully, but it's amazing how kids can get out of your sight so quickly. And when Sophia disappears for a minute or two, anything can happen. One time when Amy was out and I was watching all the kids, I remember seeing Sophia on the floor playing with some of her building blocks. Well I got busy with Evan for a moment and, all of a sudden, I smelled electrical smoke. So I started looking around and I saw that Sophia had taken my car key and had been sticking it in one of the electrical outlets. She had melted the ridges on the key and blown out the socket, and the wall just above the outlet was black. I was amazed that she hadn't been hurt. But it turned out she was fine. It wasn't hard to get an electrician to repair the wall. But I was left with two slightly more difficult problems. First, I couldn't drive my car because the key wouldn't work anymore. And second, I had to explain to Amy how I had let her baby get away and almost electrocute herself.

Sophia and Philip are very, very close. When she was one year old, we could tell that she was going to be a strong-willed child—just like Philip used to be.

And sure enough, the two of them have butted heads a number of times.

Mary Mickelson, Phil's Mom

One afternoon, when it was time for Sophia's nap, she started misbehaving. "Now, Sophia," I said, "we can't be acting

like this. Why don't we lie down for a little while and take a nap."
So I put her in her crib and, as I left, she started screaming bloody
murder.

"Sophia, if you keep this up, I'm going to have to take away
your little friends" (her stuffed animals). Well, she kept it up and I
came back in the room and took her friends away.

"Now Sophia, if you keep acting like this, I'm going to have to
take your silkies away. I don't want to, but it's your choice." So I left
and she just screamed louder and louder. Then I went back in and
took her silkies.

"Sophia, all you have left is your pacifier. Please don't make
me take your pacifier. Please stop crying. Now I'm going to leave
and come back in a little while. Hopefully, you'll stop crying and
you can keep your pacifier." This time I stood right outside the
door to see if she was going to settle down. But she just screamed
louder and louder. So I walked back into the room.

"Now Sophia," I said—and before I could finish my sentence,
Sophia stood up in the crib like the Statue of Liberty, whipped
the pacifier out of her mouth, stuck her arm out, and handed it
to me.

Well, I took it, walked out of the room, and put the pacifier at
the foot of our bed where her friends and her silkies were. Then I
went into the living room and sat down with Amy. Of course,
Sophia kept on screaming.

"What happened?" Amy asked.

"I took away all of her magic—her friends, her silkies, even her
pacifier. And she's still screaming."

"Well," replied Amy, "let's wait a few minutes and see if she set-
tles down."

Sure enough, a few minutes went by, and we heard no more noise coming out of Sophia's room. I waited a good long time to make certain that she had fallen asleep before I went into her room. I was going to cover her with a blanket. But when I walked into the room, I saw that the crib was filled with her stuffed animals, all her silkies, and the pacifier was in her mouth.

Amanda had been next door in her own room when all of this was going on. And when I left for the last time, she had apparently gone into our room, grabbed all of the magic and brought it in to her little sister. And that's why Sophia finally calmed down.

The magic was back.

When I get up to the green, I hear that Ernie has put his drive in the fairway bunker on #18. He's now unlikely to make a birdie. If I can make this putt, I'll be tied for the lead.

The 16th green sits down in a little bowl and tends to have an amphitheater effect. And when something good happens there, the sound the fans make, the roar, vibrates the entire premises. When Jack Nicklaus and Tom Watson played together here in 1991 (I was an amateur at the time), they both had putts from down on the tier to a top-right pin. Well, they both made their 50-footers with both balls curling into the side of the cup. I was up in the clubhouse at the time and I had never heard such thunderous roars before. The sounds reverberated like flocks of birds flying across the tops of the pine trees. They were continuous, rumbling roars that gradually faded into the distant reaches of the golf course.

With putter in hand, I walk around this hole and look at the break from all different angles.

Sometimes, I help read greens for Phil. But he knows this hole so well that I just went over and stood to the side of the green. At this point, I'm a spectator just like everybody else.

Jim (Bones) Mackay, Phil's Caddy

This is a great putt to have because I can be aggressive. Before I make my stroke, I get behind the ball and take one last look. I lean my head a little bit to the left—then a little bit to the right. I'm pretty sure this ball will break left six or eight inches.

I remember one day when Philip was in high school. He was sitting in class and staring at the floor. He would move his head and look at a certain spot in different ways. He'd lean left and he'd lean right. Finally, his teacher called him up to the front of the class.

"Philip, you're not paying attention," she said. "What are you staring at?"

"Well, ma'am," he replied, "I'm trying to figure out the break. If I was to roll a golf ball on the floor to that spot over there, I'm trying to figure out which way it would roll."

Philip would also roll a marble down the aisle when he was in church, just to see which way it would move. And I once saw him roll a golf ball down the aisle of an airplane in flight. "You see, Mom," he said. "You don't have to hit it very hard. The momentum of the plane will take it all the way to the back."

Mary Mickelson

___

At this point, it was very hard to see the green. People were everywhere. And some of the fans were climbing trees so they could get a good view. There was a man who climbed up this tree behind me. And the marshal came over and told him to get down. "I'm not coming down until Phil putts!" he shouted.

Then the man in the tree looked down at me and said: "You're Mrs. Mickelson, aren't you?"

"Yes," I said.

"Can you see?"

"Well, no. But I don't want to see."

"It's okay, Mrs. Mickelson," he said. "I'll tell you what happens."

And the marshal again said: "Get down out of that tree!"

And he said again: "I'm not coming down until Phil putts."

People were running all over the place, pushing toward the green. At the Masters, you're not supposed to run. And they advise you how to clap politely. Well, not this day. People were running and yelling and screaming. It was bedlam.

I closed my eyes, held my hands together, and talked to my father. "Dad, where are you? Help him. Please, help him."

Mary Mickelson

___

As I step up to the ball, everyone gets very quiet. You can hear birds chirping as I make my stroke. I hit it with a lot of pace. And people start yelling, "Get in the hole! Get in the hole!" But I don't hear them.

The putt goes directly into the center of the hole. Birdie!

I pump my fist. "Oh, baby!" I say. "Wow!"

And then I notice the roar. The ground vibrates and surges into my body! What a feeling!

I heard the huge roar and I looked up at the man in the tree. "He *birdied* it! He *birdied* it!" he shouted. Then he jumped down out of the tree and took off running toward the 17th hole, yelling: "He's gonna *do* it! He's gonna *do* it!"

Mary Mickelson

After Phil birdied #14, I grabbed the kids and drove to the golf course. We were in the parking lot walking to the clubhouse when I heard the roar. "That was an eagle roar," I thought to myself. I knew something magical was happening. I just hoped it was Phil.

Renee McBride

To say that I'm pumped up is an understatement. I have finally caught Ernie. Tied with two holes to go.

Now it's time to win.

After Phil made that putt, he came over to me and gave me a nudge. "Let's get one more, Bones," he said. He had this unbelievable look in his eye. I just knew he was going to do it.

Jim (Bones) Mackay, Phil's Caddy

PLAYER	SCORE	HOLE
Els	−8	17
Mickelson	−8	16
Choi	−6	17
DiMarco	−4	16
Langer	−4	16

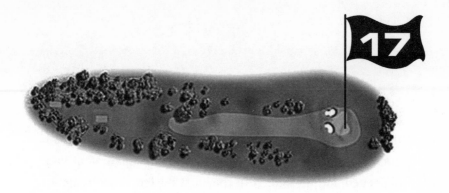

Nandina
Par 4
425 Yards

F or these last two holes, I know I really need to find the fairway
on my drives. Here on the 17th, I definitely do not want to be
right in the trees with a bad angle to the pin. So I'm going to
take my driver, aim down the right side, and hit a high fade. This will be
very similar to the tee shots I hit at #1, #9, and #14 earlier in the day.

Again, I rip this shot just as hard as I can. It sails past the Eisenhower tree—which is 195 yards out and named for President
Dwight D. Eisenhower because he always hit behind it and never
had a shot to the green. The ball goes about 310 yards, lands safely
in the fairway, and leaves me a pitching wedge to the green.

Perfect. Just where I want to be.

About this time, we heard this tremendous roar coming from the direction of the 18th green and we thought Ernie had birdied the hole. So we asked one of the marshals what had happened and he said: "Oh, they just posted Phil's birdie at #16 and they're cheering for him."

Amy Mickelson

As I'm walking down the 17th fairway, everybody's rushing forward to get a good view. I can sense all the commotion and excitement and am flattered to feel such support. But I still don't completely understand why people feel the way they do about me.

When I was still a single guy, I used to eat breakfast at this little waffle house down the road from my place. I'd go there five days a week, grab a newspaper, and eat. After a while, all the waitresses got to know me.

One weekend, Phil was staying with me before a golf tournament and we went down to the waffle house to eat. When I walked in, everybody said, "Hi, Jim. How're you doing?" "Fine," I said. I introduced Phil to everybody and we had a nice breakfast.

Phil picked up the check that morning (which was about $12). As we walked out of the place, our waitress started running after us. "Phil, you made a mistake," she said, ready to give back his hundred-dollar bill. "No, that's your tip," he said.

Well, after that, when I'd go down to the waffle house, it was never, "Hey, how're you doing, Jim?" Rather, it was always, "Where's Phil?" "When is Phil coming back?"

I asked Phil one time why he gives those big tips to kids and to waiters in restaurants. "Because they work hard for a living," he said. "They don't make much and they don't expect much, either. I make a great living and I can afford to do it. I also like to do it. It's especially nice to see a kid's eyes brighten up. It's fun for me. I like to make people happy.'"

Jim (Bones) Mackay, Phil's Caddy

My wife, Linda, and I had been married twenty-four years. I casually happened to mention to Phil that we were thinking about renewing our wedding vows on our 25th anniversary.

A month before that anniversary, Phil and Amy invited us to fly down to Mexico with them for a few days. When we got down there, we found that they had arranged for all of our family and closest friends to fly in. And they had planned this beautiful, once-in-a-lifetime wedding ceremony for us. It was a complete and total surprise—one of the most moving experiences of my life.

Whenever people ask me what kind of people Phil and Amy Mickelson are, I tell them that story.

Coach Steve Loy, Phil's Business Manager

For my approach shot, I'm thinking that I just need to make one birdie—just one. But I simply cannot miss this ball to the right because that's the only place where the ball will catch the edge and funnel off the right side of the green. So I aim just a few feet left of the pin—and I club down slightly because, with my adrenaline flowing like it is, I don't want to be long.

My swing feels very good and I think this ball is going to land perfectly. However, it flies slightly longer than I want it to, takes a huge bounce, and rolls 35 feet past the pin and stops on the high part of the green. "Uh, oh," I think. "It's lightning fast from up there."

Years ago, Ben Crenshaw showed me how fast this putt really is. He also pointed out to me how it breaks to the left instead of to the right like a lot of people think. Now I'm thinking that I just need to two-putt this, make par, and then go to #18 and make my birdie there.

Once again, as I stand over the ball, the crowd suddenly gets very quiet. All you can hear are the birds chirping in the trees. I aim about three feet to the right of the cup and just barely tap this ball. It rolls and rolls and rolls. When it is six feet out, I think it's going to go in. But it suddenly loses speed, falls off slightly to the left, and stops two feet by the hole.

It's within my circle, but I don't take it for granted. I knock it in for par.

Walking up to the 18th tee, I see that Ernie has made par and completed his round.

Okay. I'm tied for the lead with one hole to go.

Now it's just the golf course and me—just like when I was a kid.

PLAYER	SCORE	HOLE
Els	−8	18
Mickelson	−8	17
Choi	−6	18
DiMarco	−4	17
Langer	−4	18

Holly
Par 4
465 yards
Dogleg Right

*T*his final hole at Augusta National is the second most difficult on the course. And there are reasons for that. First, it's almost all uphill. Second, there are two fairway bunkers on the left side about 300 yards out (at the elbow of the dogleg). Third, you have to drive through a very narrow chute of trees. Clearly, the most critical shot on #18 is the tee shot. If you hit it in the trees right or left, you're going to be fighting for par. But if you drive it in the fairway, you'll be thinking birdie. Today, the pin is in the lower left portion of the green—and that is a great placement.

Rather than hit a driver, I pull out my 3-wood to get a little more accuracy and to be certain the ball doesn't reach the fairway bunkers. And I've also been hitting this club well all week long.

Using the 3-wood was a very smart shot. Very smart. Phil is a much better player now than he used to be—not because he hits better shots, but because he doesn't hit as many bad shots. He's hitting smarter shots. He's not going to beat himself as much as he used to.

Dave Pelz

I tee the ball up on the left side and just rip it as hard as I can. The ball goes 303 yards and lands right in the middle of the fairway. Nice.

That tee shot was one of the greatest shots I've ever seen Phil hit. Such a good shot, such a good swing. That ball went so far, it actually stopped a couple of yards past the fairway bunkers.

Coach Steve Loy

My approach shot is going to be all uphill to a two-tiered green that slopes from back to front. It's guarded by two front bunkers, one short left and one right. When I get up to the ball, I have to wait a few minutes for Bernhard Langer and Paul Casey to finish putting. I have plenty of time to think about this shot, so Bones and I discuss it in some detail.

It's 162 yards to the pin. Behind the pin, there's a little catch basin that will funnel the ball toward the hole. I have a huge margin of error. I want to hit a shot just to the right of the hole so as to catch that basin and let the ball funnel back down to the pin. I know it's a quick putt down the hill from there—but it levels off right near the cup, so there's no real threat of running it five feet by and three-putting. I've seen a lot of guys make that putt to win by one or two strokes. Vijay Singh, Mark O'Meara, and Tiger Woods all did it. Bones and I both agree on club selection. It'll be a full 8-iron.

I'm thinking I'd much rather win the tournament right here and avoid a playoff. So I let "Old Phil" step up to the ball and go for the pin. My swing feels good. The ball fades a little like I want it to. It lands six feet right of the hole, catches the basin, and stops 18 feet away from the pin. Perfect!

The walk up to the 18th green on Sunday at the Masters is a big moment for a golfer. All the spectators have gathered from all over the course. We're in the last group and there's no one else playing golf at Augusta National.

The fairway is long and uphill. People are lined up ten to fifteen deep on both sides. As I start my walk, they're all applauding and cheering. It's an impressive sight and a wonderful moment.

When I saw my son walking up the 18th fairway, I thought back to when he was nine years old and had called me out of the kitchen on Masters Sunday.

"You see, Mom," he said, "one day that's going to be me—and they're going to be clapping and yelling for me! I'm going to win the Masters and be walking up to the 18th green just like that!"

Mary Mickelson

185

I look into the crowd and see the faces of many people who are at Augusta year in and year out. It just makes me feel great—and all I can think of is to just enjoy the moment. Just enjoy it. So as I head up the hill, I smile and nod, thank you. I smile and nod.

While I was replacing the divot, Phil got about 30 yards in front of me. Standing there watching him walk up to the 18th green, I noticed that it's much more uphill than you think. The green sits way up on top of a hill.

Jim (Bones) Mackay

During that walk, I recalled the first time I took Philip to the big golf course. He was only three years old and didn't want to play the 18th hole because it would be the end of our round. I told him we had to play it—and he ran right up Cardiac Hill just as fast as he could.

"I remember thinking at that moment: "This kid is just *destined* to play golf."

Phil Mickelson, Sr.

When I get up to the green, I mark my ball and step back out of the way so that Chris DiMarco can hit out of the left front bunker. Unfortunately, just as I had done back on #5, Chris leaves his ball in the bunker. Boy, is that sand tough! Chris doesn't waste any time with his

186

next shot. I'm sure he wants neither to disrupt my concentration nor to leave his ball in the bunker again, so he steps right up and takes another swing.

This time his ball pops out, lands on the green, rolls by the pin, and comes to rest about three inches behind my mark. Of course, that means that Chris will hit first—and I will get an absolutely perfect look at how my own putt will break. Talk about luck!

As soon as that ball came of the bunker, Phil went right over and moved his mark so that Chris would be able to putt. It was my responsibility to clean DiMarco's ball because his caddy was raking out the bunker. So I went over, got the ball from Chris, and was cleaning it. All three of us were grinning. Everybody knew what this meant!

Jim (Bones) Mackay

When I came around to mark my ball, Phil tapped me on the back and said: "Show me something!"

"You got it," I said.

To tell you the truth, I didn't think there was any way Phil was going to miss that putt. It just seemed to be his time.

Chris DiMarco

While Chris is lining up his putt, I stand quietly off the edge of the green to his back right. As soon as he strokes it, I walk behind him to see what the ball will do. It breaks left, but misses the cup, and rolls about a foot by. Chris taps in. Now it's my turn.

Just as Phil was lining up his putt, I was taking the children from the family room in the clubhouse over to the scorer's hut near the 18th green. I walked by the practice green and saw Ernie Els munching on an apple. "If Phil misses his birdie putt and makes par," I thought, "then he and Ernie will be in a playoff."

Renee McBride

This is what it all comes down to, doesn't it? One downhill right-to-left putt. The last golfer to win the Masters with a birdie putt on the 18th green was Mark O'Meara in 1998. The first golfer to do it was Arnold Palmer in 1960.

On all my previous putts today, I've walked around the hole and taken a good look from all angles. But because I've seen Chris's putt, I know precisely how it's going to break. So I just stand behind the ball, visualize it rolling down the line at the right speed, and see it going into the hole.

Then I step up and take one practice stroke. It's a fairly quick downhill putt. I'm going to allow six inches of break and stroke the ball firmly.

Everyone and everything is very quiet. I don't even hear the birds chirping at this point.

I hit the putt. It feels good.

People all around the green stand up and start yelling. "Go in the hole!" "Get in the hole!" "C'mon." "C'mon." "In." "In."

I was standing off the side of the green by the scorer's hut. I closed my eyes and clenched hands with my family.

Amy Mickelson

I closed my eyes while that putt was rolling toward the hole. "Dad, help him," I said to Phil's grandfather. "Just help him. C'mon, Dad. C'mon, Dad."

Mary Mickelson

It's a quick putt, but it seems like the ball is taking forever to get there. It starts out right on my intended line. But will it hang in there for those last four feet or so? When it gets a foot from the hole, it starts to tail a bit to the left and looks like it is going to miss. But it hangs on, and hangs on, and hangs on.

My ball catches the left lip of the cup, slides along the edge all the way over to the right side—and falls into the hole. Birdie!

In the first split-second of that moment, I really believe that my grandfather nudged my ball back to the right just in the nick of time.

I was so excited I jumped up from my flat-footed position six feet above the surface of the green! With my arms and legs extended, and my putter still in my hand, I must have hung in the air for seven seconds.

And everybody else was screaming and yelling and wailing and shouting and smiling—and they had their arms over their heads, too.

———

We received letters and phone calls from people all over the nation about what they were doing and what happened when Phil made that putt. On airplanes, the pilots announced that Phil had won the Masters and passengers shouted, cheered, and cried. At the San Diego airport, people poured out of the bars into the concourses with their fists pumping, high-fives flying, and screaming in celebration. In restaurants where there were televisions, diners started applauding and yelling. Just outside Phil's childhood home, a neighbor was out in his front yard when he heard roars coming from the inside of four or five houses on his street. One guy from the Midwest wrote us that he jumped so high, when he came down he actually broke his leg! Others said they could now go eat their Easter dinners.

Gary McBride, Amy's Dad

———

When I finally float down to the ground from my Olympic-caliber, NBA-worthy leap, the first thing I do is walk over to Bones, give him a great big hug, and say: "I did it! I did it!"

"You did it! You did it!" he shouts back. Chris DiMarco gives me a high-five and a pat on the back. "Way to go, Phil!"

I walk over to the hole, pull out my golf ball, kiss it, and toss it into the crowd. The people are still screaming, shouting, smiling, and crying. I hand my putter to Bones, who takes it and, along with the flagstick, puts it in my golf bag. I walk through the crowd toward the scorer's hut. People are holding out their hands and I give them high fives. One, two, three, four, five . . . ten high fives in all.

When I get up there, I see Amy. She jumps into my arms and I give her the biggest hug and kiss. She can't speak. She's crying. I see my mom, my dad, my sister, Amy's mom, and Amy's dad. I give them each a hug, look them in the eye, and say, "I did it! I did it!"

My dad leans in and says, "I'm proud of you, son."

I see Steve Loy and give him a bear hug. I'm just about to walk up the steps into the scorer's hut when I hear, "Daddy! Daddy!" It's Amanda calling to me.

I turn around and pick her up. "Amanda, I did it!" I say to her. "Can you believe it?"

He was really excited. He wants to win every tournament and he almost does. I told him I was surprised that he won. Then I gave him a great big hug. I was holding on to his neck and he squeezed me so tight.

Amanda Mickelson, Phil's Daughter

Then I see Sophia. I pick her up and hold her in my arms. "Sophia," I say. "Daddy won! Can you believe it?"

Then I go over to Amy. She's holding our son, Evan, who's just turned one year old. At that moment, I feel so blessed to be Amanda, Sophia, and Evan's dad—and to have them with me.

Phil, you're going to be a father and there's nothing greater in the world.

Payne Stewart, 1999 U.S. Open Champion

Okay, now I've hugged and kissed everybody and it's time to walk up into the scorer's hut. But before I go, I take one look back at Amy. She sees me and we make eye contact. It was just for a moment, but it means so much for me to see her standing there holding Evan. After all we had gone through in 2003, after almost losing them both, here they are sharing in this wonderful, almost miraculous moment. And I realize that winning the Masters, as great as it feels, isn't the most important thing in my life.

In the scorer's hut, all I can think about is to make sure the scorecard I sign is correct. I was thinking about Roberto de Vicenzo who, back in 1968, had signed an incorrect card. He finished in a tie but mistakenly marked his birdie at #17 as a par and lost the tournament by one shot. Bob Goalby got the green jacket that year. "What a stupid I am," said de Vicenzo to the press afterwards.

So I look over my card carefully with Bones and Chris DiMarco. Front nine: 4, 4, 5, 3, 5, 4, 4, 5, 4. Two over par 38. Check. Back nine: 4, 4, 2, 4, 3, 5, 2, 4, 3. A scorching 31 with five birdies. Check. Overall, a three under par 69. Check. Grand total of 279, nine under par for

the tournament. I win the Masters by one shot. It's my twenty-third ca-
reer victory—and my first major.

After Phil went into the scorer's hut, a reporter came over and
wanted to interview me. But I was too emotional to even speak.
So he asked if he could interview Amanda. I nodded yes.

"Amanda, is this the greatest day of your life?" he asked.

"Yes, it is," she replied.

"Is it the greatest day of your life because your daddy
won the Masters?"

"No, it's the greatest day because we colored Easter eggs
this morning."

Amy Mickelson

Just as I finish signing my scorecard, I take a moment to relax. The
scorer's hut is right next to the practice green at the clubhouse. So we've
come full circle and we're right back where we started. Somebody else
walks through the door and Sophia just follows him right in. She likes to
cling to me, and I love that. I pick her up, put her in my lap, and she
cups my face in her hand. "I love you, Daddy," she says—her big round
eyes melting my heart. Then we turn to the right and look out the win-
dow. Everybody is smiling and waving at us. I point to Amy and say,
"Wave to the people, Sophia."

At first she doesn't wave. So I take the pacifier out of her mouth and
say, "Wave." Sophia, who is right-handed, now smiles and waves with
her left hand. Then she takes the pacifier away from me and puts it back
in her mouth.

I waved because I was happy. I waved because my daddy is my daddy.

Sophia Mickelson, Phil's Daughter

I've won the Masters. Sophia is sitting in my lap. She has her magic back. And all is right with the world.

PLAYER	SCORE	TOTAL
Phil Mickelson	−9	279
Ernie Els	−8	280
K. J. Choi	−6	282
Sergio Garcia	−3	285
Bernhard Langer	−3	285
Paul Casey	−2	286
Fred Couples	−2	286
Chris DiMarco	−2	286
Davis Love III	−2	286
Nick Price	−2	286
Vijay Singh	−2	286
Kirk Triplett	−2	286
Retief Goosen	E	288
Padraig Harrington	E	288
Charles Howell III	E	288
Casey Wittenberg	E	288*

*(Low Amateur)

19th Hole

After signing my scorecard, I was escorted over to the Butler Cabin for the formal green jacket ceremony. The tradition is that the previous year's Masters champ holds the green jacket for the new champ. That honor fell to Mike Weir (who is also a lefty). As he held out my size 43L jacket, I slipped it on, and said exactly what I was feeling. "I can't believe this is happening," I remarked. "It's the fulfillment of dreams. I'm just proud to be a champion here. It was an exceptional back nine, and it's something I'll remember forever and ever."

It *was* an exceptional day. In particular, it was very meaningful for me to win the Masters during Arnold Palmer's final competitive appearance here. I couldn't help but think back to the letter he wrote to me after the 2002 Bay Hill Invitational. "You never would have won as many tournaments as you have by playing a more conservative game," he wrote. "Keep playing to win. Keep charging. Your majors will come." Mr. Palmer was known for his charges on the back nine at Augusta—and I believe I won in a way that would have made him proud.

My colleagues on the Tour also seemed to be caught up in Sunday's drama. I think Paul Casey, who was playing in the group ahead of me, said it best. "It's rare I become interested in what's happening if I'm not in the lead," he said. "But today, I was genuinely interested in what was going on out there. You become a fan as much as a golfer for a while. It was remarkable stuff."

I was also touched by the graciousness of Ernie Els. He had shot a magnificent five under par round of 67. Nobody makes two eagles coming down the stretch at Augusta on Sunday and doesn't win. And yet, when the tournament was taken away from him on the 18th green, he handled himself with great class and showed that he was genuinely happy for me.

I played as well as I can. What more could I do? I think Phil deserved this one. The man upstairs was there for him. He earned it. Full credit to him.

Ernie Els

Back at the main clubhouse, as we were preparing to go in for the formal Masters dinner, I received a call from President George W. Bush. He congratulated me and said that his entire staff jumped up from their seats when I made that final putt. And then he ribbed me a little bit. "Now I know why you play golf instead of basketball," he said. "You can't dunk!"

After that call, Phil came out with a big grin on his face and told the rest of us: "The President just roughed me up about my jump! He must not have seen me at my apex."

Amy Mickelson

The formal dinner had a wonderfully festive atmosphere. Just before we walked in Amanda went around telling everybody that green was her new favorite color. As we ate, people offered all kinds of toasts. And when everybody ran out of eloquent words, we would just hold up their glasses and yell, "Yeeeee, haaaa!" It was unforgettable.

Afterward, all our family and friends joined us at our rental house and we continued the celebration. I changed into something more comfortable: black workout shorts, a black T-shirt, and an ASU baseball cap. But I kept my green jacket on. And I looked *good*! We played Ping-Pong, told stories, and generally relived the day. And when it was finally time to settle down, the three of us went to bed together: Amy, me, and the green jacket. The next morning, bright and early, Sophia came into our room and snuggled up inside the jacket. It has a lining similar to her "silkie" blanket and she loved the feel of it. "Daddy, you won the green jacket!" she said, giving me a high-five. "Great job!"

Over the next several weeks, I went on a coast-to-coast media trip—appearing on the Jay Leno and David Letterman shows, among others. I was even asked to ring the opening bell on the floor of the New York Stock Exchange. What a moment that was! I felt like a prize fighter entering the ring. People were slapping me on the back and the traders on the floor treated me great. I also received countless notes and letters of congratulations from people all across the nation, including many golfing greats. One particularly touching one came from Bryon Nelson. "Wow! Wasn't that the most exciting finish that I ever saw! After the great four at #10, you were turned on. You played so fine and looked so happy. Your family looked great. Please hug them for me."

Bones and his wife, Jen, had their baby four days after the

Masters—a healthy, strong boy they named Oliver. Rick Smith and his wife, Tricia (our good friend and vegetarian), flew out to visit us and we took them to our favorite burger joint, *In-N-Out.* She had told us that if I won the Masters she would eat meat. So she ordered a double-double and ate the whole thing. When we finally got home, some of my friends threw a surprise party for me. People showed up from all over the country to help us celebrate.

Later, the people at Augusta asked me to follow the tradition of sending them the one club in my bag that most helped me win the Masters. So I sent them the 8-iron I had used on my approach shots to #12, #16, and #18—all of which I birdied.

The remainder of the 2004 golf season went very well for me. With regard to the three other majors, I finished second in the U.S. Open, third in the British Open, and sixth in the PGA Championship. Actually, I came within a total of five strokes of winning them all.

During the year, of course, there was still some discussion about my previous drought in the majors. For instance, I was asked this question: "Phil, what would you have thought about your career without a major?"

"I've never thought about that," I responded. "Nor do I have to!"

That's the absolute truth. I never really did worry about not winning a major. I knew that time and history were on my side. After all, Sam Snead won twenty-seven tournaments before claiming his first major victory. And Ben Hogan, of all people, won thirty. So I felt pretty optimistic that I'd eventually break through. Nobody can win the Masters or the other majors all the time. You only have the magic once in awhile. And besides, the greater the challenge, the more rewarding the victory.

One thing I was not prepared for, however, was the widespread reaction to my first major victory. People all over the nation reacted emotionally and celebrated as if they had won it themselves. My own family remained on an emotional high for at least a month.

Our entire family was emotional for weeks after the Masters. The only person who didn't cry was Phil—and he never shed a tear.

Amy Mickelson

I've given a lot of thought to why so many people reacted so enthusiastically to my win at the Masters. Part of the reason, I think, is that we all have something in common. We're all trying to win our own personal major. Every day, we work hard to make a little progress. And every day, we get beaten back a little bit.

It's not easy to win a major, or achieve a dream, or make it to that magic destination where we believe success lies. Now that I've finally made it, I can tell you one very important thing I've learned along the way. And that is that the real magic is not so much in achieving the victory, itself. The *real* magic is in *the journey* we take to get there.

I'll always cherish the green jacket, but the real prize for me was hitting a thousand shots on the driving range with Rick Smith, stroking a thousand putts on the green with Dave Pelz, and making five birdies on the back nine at Augusta.

The real prize is not the beautiful Masters trophy sitting on my shelf at home. The real prize was hitting a thousand chip shots in the backyard with my dad, skipping a ball off the water with Coach Steve Loy as my caddy, and hitting a thousand golf balls by myself in the rain.

I was fortunate to win the Masters. But I'm more fortunate to have a great life partner in my wife, Amy, with whom I share everything. I was blessed with a natural golf swing. But I'm more blessed to have three healthy and loving children in my life—Amanda, Sophia, and Evan.

To win my first major without my family around would have been unthinkable. To win it with them there, to share in that wonderful moment with me, made it absolutely priceless.

Like many other good things in my life that have come back to me, the ball I threw into the crowd from the 18th green was returned by the fan who caught it. I took that ball and the flag from the 18th pin and had them framed together in a glass case. Then I gave it to my grandmother. It now hangs on the wall of my grandfather's kitchen. A major flag with all his other tournament flags. Just like he wanted.

When Evan was about 18 months old, he spent the day over at my parents' house. Dad took him out to the backyard green and gave him a sawed off kid's putter and some golf balls to play with. He spent the better part of the day out there. And when it came time for him to come in and eat, he wouldn't leave the back yard. My mom says that's exactly the way I acted when I was his age.

Amy sometimes wears a small bracelet on her wrist. It's a circle with three charms on it. Joy for Evan. Patience for Sophia. Peace for Amanda.

As in golf, life is a game of circles.

Acknowledgments

We'd like to thank Larry Kirshbaum and Rick Wolff at the Time Warner Book Group for their insight, encouragement, and enthusiasm during this project. Steve Loy and Bob Barnett, our agents, are the best in the world at what they do and deserve credit for pulling everything together as quickly as they did.

We are also indebted to the following people for their insights, interviews, and support: Mary and Philip Mickelson, Sr., Tina Mickelson, Tim Mickelson, Renee and Gary McBride, Steve Loy, Jim (Bones) Mackay, Dave Pelz, Rick Smith, Amanda Mickelson, Sophia Mickelson, Evan Mickelson, Hevin ZaZa, and T. R. Reinman. At the Time Warner Book Group, we would also like to thank Jason Pinter, Bob Castillo, Thomas Whatley, and Jim Spivey, as well as Ellen Rosenblatt of SD Designs.

A very special acknowledgment must go to Amy Mickelson, who participated in every step of the writing, editing, and creative process. She's a full partner in this effort. Thanks, Amy.

Phil Mickelson
Don Phillips

About Donald T. Phillips

Don Phillips is a best-selling author of major works of nonfiction. His trilogy on American leadership (*The Founding Fathers on Leadership*, *Lincoln on Leadership*, and *Martin Luther King Jr. on Leadership*) has won worldwide acclaim. His first book, *Lincoln on Leadership*, paved the way toward the creation of an entire new genre of books on historical leadership. Mr. Phillips has also collaborated on two books with legendary basketball coach Mike (Coach K) Krzyzewski of Duke University (*Leading with the Heart*, and *Five-Point Play*). *One Magical Sunday* is his fourteenth book.

BOOKS BY DONALD T. PHILLIPS

Lincoln on Leadership (Warner Books, 1992)

On the Brink: The Life and Leadership of Norman Brinker (with Norman Brinker; Summit, 1996)

Lincoln Stories for Leaders (Summit, 1997)

The Founding Fathers on Leadership (Warner Books, 1997)

Martin Luther King Jr. on Leadership (Warner Books, 1999)

A Diamond in Spring (Summit, 1999)

Leading with the Heart: Coach K's Successful Strategies in Basketball, Business, and Life (with Mike Krzyzewski; Warner Books, 2000)

Run to Win: Vince Lombardi on Coaching and Leadership (St. Martin's Press, 2001)

Five-Point Play: The Story of Duke's Amazing 2000–2001 Championship Season (with Mike Krzyzewski; Warner Books, 2001)

Unto Us a Child: Abuse and Deception in the Catholic Church (Tapestry Press, 2002)

Character in Action: The U.S. Coast Guard on Leadership (with Admiral James M. Loy; Naval Institute Press, 2003)

Disasters: Insights and Impacts (with Randall Bell; Tapestry Press, 2005)

The Rudy in You: A Youth Sports Guide for Players, Parents, and Coaches (with Rudy Ruettiger and Peter Leddy; Bonus Books, 2005)